THE
EVERTON
MISCELLANY

THE
EVERTON
MISCELLANY

BY MARK O'BRIEN

VSP

Vision Sports Publishing
2 Coombe Gardens,
London SW20 0QU

www.visionsp.co.uk

Published by Vision Sports Publishing 2008

Text © Mark O'Brien
Illustrations © Bob Bond Sporting Caricatures

ISBN 13: 978-1-905326-19-8

Printed and bound in Germany by
GGP Media GmbH, Pössneck

Typeset by Palimpsest Book Production Limited,
Grangemouth, Stirlingshire

A CIP catalogue record for this book is
available from the British Library

Foreword
By Graeme Sharp

During my 25-year association with Everton, firstly as a player and then in my role as Fans' Liaison Officer and now Charities' Manager, it's become very clear to me that the supporters of this club are fiercely proud of its history and traditions.

As founder member of the Football League, the Blues actually have a longer history than most – something that becomes abundantly clear when reading this excellent book of facts and figures from every era, from the present where they are led by David Moyes in the Premier League, and stretching back to the earliest days when they where still a church team called St Domingo's.

Obviously I had heard of Everton before I moved down south from Scotland. I'd taken an interest in Bob Latchford, because he was a striker like myself, and I knew about some of the Scottish boys like Asa Hartford, but it was only when I first visited, prior to my move from Dumbarton, that I got a real sense of the size of the club. Training has moved to even better facilities at Finch Farm only recently, and much has been made of the way that Goodison Park is showing its age, but back in 1981 the training ground at Bellefield and the famous old stadium itself were mightily impressive.

I never hesitated in making the move and even though I struggled a bit at first, along with the rest of a relatively young side, and I probably was a bit homesick at times, I never wanted to leave, even when there was talk of Alex Ferguson wanting me up at Aberdeen. And how glad I am that I did remain here as well, because once Peter Reid arrived, as well as Andy Gray – who was my hero, even though he hates me saying that! – we developed a confidence that we had lacked in the past and went on to enjoy some of the most successful years in the club's history.

I consider myself really lucky to have been a part of an era that the fans still remember so vividly and fondly, and reading here about some of those famous games from the eighties brings back great memories for me. There were the cup finals, the matches that clinched league titles, the European matches and, of course, the big encounters with our closest rivals across the park.

Everyone warned me about the atmosphere in the Merseyside derbies but I was perhaps a bit blasé at first after watching Old Firm games and thinking that they couldn't be as intense. It wasn't until I took to the pitch in my first one though, and the noise from the crowd hit me, that I realised that although these games thankfully lacked the religious edge of the Glasgow clashes, they were every bit as passionate.

I actually scored in that first derby match, but we lost 3–1, and there was probably always a bit of a feeling that we couldn't beat Liverpool's all-conquering side, full of established household names. That changed over time, and although people still mention my goal at Anfield in 1984, I always stress that while of course it was nice to net a spectacular effort like that, the most important thing about that day was that it made everyone realise that we could beat them and that we actually had no reason to fear anyone.

To this day though, I have to confess I would far rather play in a derby game than watch one.

The club haven't always enjoyed the best of times since Howard Kendall's first spell in charge and I've been as disappointed as anyone when I've seen Everton struggling at the wrong end of the table. I like to think it goes without saying that I've really felt for the supporters when things have been tough, because they have always been so magnificent and have really helped Everton through some of those lean spells. It's been great then to see how things seem to have turned around under the present manager, a fellow Scot, David Moyes, who has been totally focussed since his arrival at Goodison where he has undoubtedly established himself as one of the very best in the game.

Hopefully he will continue to lead Everton in the right direction and his sides can produce more great matches and memorable moments like some of those detailed here in *The Everton Miscellany*.

Graeme Sharp

Acknowledgements

Firstly, a thanks to Jim Drewett and everyone at VSP for asking me to write the book, and Andy Mitten for suggesting me to them in the first place.

A nod also to all the people who put in the time and the effort to produce the books, websites, fanzines and magazines about Everton that keep the supporters consistently informed and entertained. In particular, the statistics from Steve Johnson's lovingly maintained website, Evertonresults.com, were absolutely priceless in putting this book together.

Thanks to my extended family, the O'Briens, Schofields and Campbells, and everyone who goes to the match with me, all the others I know from various alehouses, particularly the Chapel and the Stuart, and everyone who contributes, in whatever way, to the *When Skies Are Grey* website and magazine. You all know who you are; I just hope you know that you are always appreciated.

Finally, thanks to Graham Ennis, Phil Redmond, Dave Wiggins and Dave Swaffield for letting me get involved with my favourite magazine all those years ago.

— THE BIRTH OF EVERTON —

1878 is officially the year in which it all began. St Domingo's Methodist Church, whose chapel opened in 1871, already ran an athletics club and cricket team for the children of the parish but were in search of some sporting activity that would also occupy them during the winter months.

They eventually decided on association football, and in 1878 St Domingo FC was formed. They played their earliest matches, exhibitions against other parish sides, in Stanley Park, the public space that still divides Goodison Park and Anfield to this day.

St Domingo's quickly established themselves as one of the leading local teams with a growing following from beyond the borders of the parish. At a meeting in the Queen's Head Hotel in November 1879, a decision was made to change the name to that of the surrounding area, and therefore St Domingo's became Everton Football Club.

— THE HONOURS —

League champions
1890/91; 1914/15; 1927/28; 1931/32; 1938/39; 1962/63; 1969/70; 1984/85; 1986/87

FA Cup winners
1906; 1933; 1966; 1984; 1995

European Cup Winners' Cup winners
1985

Second Division champions
1930/31

FA Charity Shield winners
1928; 1932; 1963; 1970; 1984; 1985; 1986 (shared); 1987; 1995

— FROM ANFIELD TO GOODISON —

After three years at Stanley Park, Everton played for a short spell at Priory Road before moving to a new home at Anfield Road in 1884. This land was owned by a pair of local businessmen, the Orrell brothers, who allowed Everton the use of their fields in the understanding that they maintained the grounds, caused no nuisance to neighbours and paid a very small rent. The club's president at the time, a brewer by the name of John Houlding, was initially the representative tenant, but he changed the rules and installed himself instead as the club's landlord.

As Everton's income increased, so did the rent they paid Houlding, to the anger of the other members of the board, particularly George Mahon, the man who would eventually lead a revolt against the man known to many as King John. At a meeting in September 1891, Houlding proposed forming a limited company to purchase the Anfield Road site from the Orrell brothers but Mahon and his supporters rejected it and proposed that Everton look for a new home instead. In reply to doubting voices from the floor, wondering if a suitable venue even existed, Mahon famously replied, "I've got one in my pocket." And in his pocket he had Mere Green Field, the piece of land that would become Goodison Park.

Undeterred by his tenants' plans to leave, Houlding attempted to register his own Everton Football Club to play at Anfield, but this was rejected by the Football Association. King John was nothing if not persistent though, and so in March 1892, to fill the void created at Anfield by Everton's move across Stanley Park, he formed Liverpool Football Club, and one of the most famous rivalries in world football duly commenced.

— COULDN'T KEEP AWAY? —

The players who had more than one spell at Everton:

	First spell	Second spell
Jack Angus	Dec 1888–Jan 1889	Aug 1890–April 1891
Bob Kelso	Jan 1889–May1889	May 1891–May 1896
Charlie Parry	July 1889–Nov 1891	Dec 1892–Nov 1895
David Kirkwood	Sept 1889–July 1891	Oct 1891–March 1892
John Bell	Aug 1892–Aug 1898	July 1901–Aug 1903
George Molyneux	March 1896–June 1897	May 1898–May 1900
Wilf Toman	April 1899–June 1900	July 1901–Jan 1904
Bert Sharp	Aug 1899–May 1900	May 1901–Aug 1904
Jack Crelley	Aug 1900–Sept 1901	Aug 1902–July 1908
Tom Corrin	Aug 1900–Aug 1901	May 1903–Aug 1904
Louis Weller	March 1910–Sept 1910	March 1911–May 1922
Ernie Gault	April 1912–Aug 1913	Aug 1917–May 1920
Howard Baker	Nov 1920–Feb 1921	July 1926–March 1929
Dave Hickson	May 1949–Sept 1955	July 1957–Nov 1959
Howard Kendall	March 1967–March 1974	May 1981–June 1987
Andy King	March 1976–Sept 1980	July 1982–July 1984
Alan Harper	June 1983–July 1988	Aug 1991–Sept 1993
David Unsworth	June 1992–Aug 1997	Aug 1998–July 2004
Duncan Ferguson	Oct 1994–Nov 1998	Aug 2000–May 2006
Alessandro Pistone	July 2000–June 2005	July 2005– May 2007
Alan Stubbs	July 2001–June 2005	Jan 2006–Jan 2008

— EVERTON LEGENDS:
WILLIAM RALPH 'DIXIE' DEAN —

The legendary Dixie Dean

When it comes to Everton players, one stands head and shoulders above all the rest. His image, leading the team out of the tunnel, is continually used as shorthand for all that is great about the club and its heritage. Indeed, a ten-foot bronze statue, unveiled on 4th May 2001, stands at the Park End of Goodison, the place where this outstanding individual set a record that has stood for 80 years and will almost certainly never be beaten. He is, of course, William Ralph 'Dixie' Dean.

Born in Birkenhead in 1907, Dean made his debut for Tranmere Rovers reserves in December 1923. He scored frequently for the Prenton Park club's second string and subsequently forced himself into the first team for the 1924/25 season. The decision to promote him to the senior squad paid off immediately as Dean scored 27 goals in 27 matches and, understandably, caught the eye of the country's biggest clubs. Those included Everton, the team that Dean supported as a boy, and in March 1925 they paid a fee of £3,000 to take the 18-year-old striker to Goodison Park.

The youngster made his debut on 21st March 1925, in a 3–1 defeat at Highbury, and saw what he believed to be a perfectly good goal disallowed – the referee claimed his effort never crossed the line. However, he wouldn't be denied for long, scoring the first of his phenomenal 383 Everton goals in the next match, a 2–0 home defeat of Aston Villa, and eventually ended that campaign as the newest royal blue idol, thanks to the 33 goals he netted, including three hat-tricks and the first of many against the enemy from across the park.

However, Dean's record-breaking career was almost cut short when he was involved in a motorcycle accident in North Wales in June 1926. The popular legend of the time had it that the doctors treating his serious injuries inserted a metal plate into his forehead and therein laid the secret of his powerful heading. Armoured noggin or not, he defied early fears and recovered sufficiently to score 24 goals during the 1926/27 season. He was, however, only warming up. In the 1927/28 season, Dean scored 60 league goals, a record that unsurprisingly still stands to this day.

He won two league titles with Everton and also scored in the FA Cup triumph over Manchester City in 1933, bundling goalkeeper Len Langford into the net in a manner that would probably earn a yellow card nowadays. He continued to score prolifically until he was sold to Notts County in 1938. He later played briefly for Sligo Rovers in the League of Ireland and then Hurst FC in Ashton before retiring in 1941.

Some might say fittingly, the greatest Everton player of all time actually passed away at Goodison Park, suffering heart failure shortly after the final whistle of a Merseyside derby in 1980.

"Those of us privileged to see Dean play talk of him the way people talk about Beethoven, Shakespeare or Mozart – he was that good."
Bill Shankly

Dixie Dean factfile
Born: Birkenhead, 22nd January 1907
Appearances: 433
Goals: 383
Other clubs: Tranmere Rovers, Notts County, Sligo Rovers, Hurst FC
Full international appearances while at Everton: 16 for England

— THE FOUNDING FATHERS —

George Mahon: The head of a prominent firm of accountants in the city, the former organist at St Domingo's Church masterminded the move from Anfield and the split with John Houlding that saw Everton move to Goodison Park and the formation of Liverpool FC.

Dr James Clement Baxter: The physician and local politician was Mahon's closest ally. When the move to Mere Green Field, ie Goodison, put the club's finances into a perilous state, Dr Baxter secured its future by way of a £1,000 interest-free loan, a massive sum in 1892. He would serve the club, as board member and chairman, for 39 years.

Will Cuff: Another staunch St Domingo's man, Cuff, a local solicitor, joined the Everton board in 1895. He became the club secretary in 1901 and served as such until 1918 when he took a three-year break to concentrate on his business. He returned, though, and was appointed chairman in 1921, a post he would hold for 17 years. He continued to serve on the board for a further ten years and only resigned in 1948, at the age of 76, after falling out with the other members. All in all, he served Everton for over 50 years and was as influential as any other figure in establishing it as one of the biggest clubs in the land.

— HANGING AROUND CORNERS —

Sam Chedgzoy enjoyed an illustrious 16-year career as an inside right with the Blues, winning a league title and eight England caps, but for all his great service his name has really become synonymous with one particular incident that occurred in 1924.

Ernest Edwards, the sports editor at the *Liverpool Echo*, noted that a recent rule change, permitting players to score directly from corners, never stipulated how many touches were allowed by the taker. Intrigued by this apparent loophole, Edwards is alleged to have offered Chedgzoy the princely sum of £2 to put the laws of the game to the test in the home match against Arsenal on 15th November.

When the Toffees won a corner Chedgzoy took it, but instead of floating a cross into the centre as normal, he dribbled the ball into the box before firing a shot past the bewildered Gunners' goalkeeper.

The referee immediately disallowed the effort, despite Chedgzoy's protestations and Everton subsequently lost the match 2–3. The FA subsequently clarified the ruling to give us the one we have today, ie another player must make contact with the ball before the corner-taker can touch it again.

— STUCK WITH A MIDDLE LIKE YOU —

Everton players with unusual middle names:

Earl **Delisser** Barrett
Daniel **Owefen** Amokachi
Drew **Scougal** Brand
Alexander 'Sandy' **Dewar** Brown
David **Desiré** Marc Ginola
Andrew **Mullen** Gray
Maurice John **Giblin** Johnston
Roger **Norton** Kenyon
Gary **Winston** Lineker
John **Morgan** Oster
Alexander **Silcock** Scott
Steven **Preben** Simonsen
Trevor **McGregor** Steven

— GOT YOUR NUMBER —

Although Arsenal and Chelsea had worn numbers on their shirts in league games back in 1928, the first time they were ever seen on a major occasion, in this case an FA Cup Final, was in 1933 when Everton faced Manchester City. For this encounter, Everton were numbered from 1 to 11, while City wore 12 to 22.

The Everton line-up was:

1. Ted Sagar
2. Billy Cook
3. Warney Cresswell
4. Cliff Britton
5. Tommy White
6. Jock Thomson
7. Albert Geldard
8. James Dunn
9. Dixie Dean (c)
10. Tommy Johnson
11. Jimmy Stein

Everton won the match 3–0 thanks to goals from Jimmy Stein, Dixie Dean and James Dunn.

— THE MAGNIFICENT SEVEN —

When Howard Kendall arrived as player-manager in the summer of 1981 he sought to rejuvenate the struggling squad with a host of new players that the local press christened the Magnificent Seven – because there were seven of them, obviously. They were:

Jim Arnold
Alan Ainscow
Alan Biley
Mick Ferguson
Neville Southall
Mickey Thomas
Mike Walsh

Unfortunately, the only one who proved in any way magnificent was the scruffy goalkeeper from Bury.

— BIG BOB'S 30 GOALS —

The 1970s was an underwhelming period in Everton's history. After winning the league in the 1969/70 season, the rest of the decade remained silverware free and was characterised by false dawns and disappointments. Evertonians were desperate for something to shout about then, and it arrived in the 1977/78 season thanks to the goalscoring form of Bob Latchford.

Signed from Birmingham City in 1974 for £350,000, in a deal that saw both Howard Kendall and Archie Styles go in the opposite direction, Latchford was a powerful frontman who carried on the tradition of the Everton number 9s with distinction and ended his Goodison career as the club's second highest scorer of all time, although he was later pushed into third by Graeme Sharp. Latchford's crowning glory came in the 1977/78 season though, when the *Daily Express* offered up a £10,000 prize to the first player to score 30 league goals.

Although the club's highest scorer in the previous three seasons, Latchford had not scored more than 20 goals in any of those campaigns. The inspired signing of England winger Dave Thomas from QPR though, with his trademark moulded studs and rolled down socks, saw a valuable new supply line open for 'the Latch' and he thrived on a stream of pinpoint crosses from the left flank.

Still, the Brummie frontman started his bid for the prize money slowly and didn't score a league goal until the fifth game, a 5–1 romp at Filbert Street. His tally was then boosted by the four goals he grabbed away at QPR in October, in another 5–1 win, and a hat-trick at home to Coventry in November did him no harm either.

Unlike Dixie Dean, who needed seven goals from the last two games of the season to reach his personal milestone back in 1928, Latchford needed just two to attain his. However, he didn't find the net in a 3–1 reverse at the Hawthorns and so it came down to the final match of the season, at home to Chelsea in front of almost 40,000 expectant Evertonians.

The Toffees put on a show for their supporters and found themselves three up but without Latchford getting on the score sheet. However, he eventually did head past Peter Bonetti to set up a grandstand finish. With ten minutes remaining in the match, and with the Blues now 5–0 ahead, Mick Lyons was fouled in the area and Latchford had the opportunity he was seeking to step up and score the crucial 30th goal of the campaign. Despite the almost unbearable tension he duly cracked his shot home from the spot, to the obvious delight of the Goodison crowd.

The newspaper's prize money was split between a donation to the Professional Footballers' Association's charities while the bulk of the rest was divvied up with the other players and staff at Everton. And Latchford's personal reward for being kicked around by defenders as he scored his 30 goals? The small remainder of the money he kept for himself apparently earned him months of grief from the taxman!

The full rundown of Latchford's goals:

Date	Opponents	Score	Goals (tally)
10th Sept 1977	Leicester (a)	3–1	1 (1)
1st Oct 1977	Man City (h)	1–1	1 (2)
4th Oct 1977	West Brom (h)	3–1	1 (3)
8th Oct 1977	QPR (a)	5–1	4 (7)
29th Oct 1977	Newcastle (h)	4–4	2 (9)
12th Nov 1977	Birmingham (h)	2–1	2 (11)
26th Nov 1977	Coventry (h)	6–0	3 (14)
3rd Dec 1977	Chelsea (a)	1–0	1 (15)
10th Dec 1977	Middlesbrough (h)	3–0	2 (17)
26th Dec 1977	Manchester United (h)	2–6	1 (18)
31st Dec 1977	Arsenal (h)	2–0	1 (19)
4th Feb 1978	Leicester (h)	2–0	2 (21)
24th March 1978	Newcastle (a)	2–0	1 (22)
25th March 1978	Leeds (h)	2–0	1 (23)
27th March 1978	Manchester United (a)	2–1	2 (25)
1st April 1978	Derby (h)	2–1	1 (26)
8th April 1978	Coventry (a)	2–3	1 (27)
15th April 1978	Ipswich (h)	1–0	1 (28)
29th April 1978	Chelsea (h)	6–0	2 (30)

— EH, DONKEY! —

When Sam Chedgzoy stretched the limits of the law with his dribble from a corner back in 1924, the referee disallowed the goal. Fast forward to 3rd October 1970 and Everton were this time on the receiving end of an equally controversial strike at Highfield Road. Needless to say though, this one stood.

With reigning champions Everton trailing 2–1, Coventry City were awarded a free kick in a good position for a dig at goal. As the Everton wall assembled, Scottish international Willie Carr stood astride the ball, before clamping it between both ankles and flicking it into the air. His teammate Ernie Hunt, who had made 14 appearances for Everton back in 1967, smashed an absolute screamer of a volley over the wall and into Andy Rankin's top corner.

Again, the laws were subsequently amended, with the FA ruling that the 'donkey kick' represented a double touch of the ball. To add insult to injury though, Hunt's strike not only stood, it also won *Match of the Day*'s Goal of the Season.

— GOING FOR GOLD —

Two Olympic gold medallists have graced the books of Everton. The most recent was Daniel Amokachi, hero of the 1995 FA Cup semi-final, who a year later was part of the Nigerian football team that caused massive upsets at the Olympics by coming from behind in both the semi-final and the final in Atlanta, beating Brazil and Argentina 4–3 and 3–2 respectively.

Back in 1908, the Games that were originally destined for Rome – but had to be moved following the eruption of Mount Vesuvius – took place in London instead. England were represented by an amateur side that contained Harold Hardman, who played for Everton as well as Blackpool, Stoke and Manchester United, without ever turning professional.

The hosts beat Denmark 2–0 in the final in White City on 24th October. Hardman also represented the full England side on four occasions and after his playing career ended enjoyed a long association with Manchester United as director and chairman.

— TWO'S A CROWD —

Ireland international Kevin Sheedy arguably conjured more memorable moments of skill during Everton's 1980s glory days than any other player. A couple of them stick out in particular though, and both of them involve distinctive doubles.

Now, you've got to be a special sort of player to cross Stanley Park and be accepted, and luckily for Sheedy, signed by Howard Kendall in August 1982, he had talent aplenty to win over the Goodison faithful. While not blessed with a great deal of pace or strength, and hardly the most industrious worker either, what Sheeds did have was a magical left foot. His crossing was a delight, and played no small part in the number of goals scored by bustling targetmen Graeme Sharp and Andy Gray. Even more potent than his pinpoint centres though was his ability to strike a dead ball. Eventually, every time the Blues gained a free kick anywhere within 40 yards of the opposition goal, the chant of "Sheedy, Sheedy, Sheedy" from the crowd would entice him to take a shot.

The most remarkable goal that Sheedy scored from a set piece came in an FA Cup sixth round tie against Ipswich on 9th March 1985. With typical precision he curled his shot over the wall and into the right-hand corner of the goal. However, much to the disappointment of the Goodison crowd, the referee said he hadn't been ready and so demanded the kick be retaken. With his second attempt, Sheedy simply tucked the ball into the opposite corner instead. Rather modestly, in an interview 20 years later, Sheedy did say that the goalkeeper Paul Cooper made the second attempt a bit easier by overcompensating with his positioning, expecting the ball to go to the right again.

On 25th April 1987, fans witnessed another Sheedy screamer and another memorable duo. It was only the one strike this time, a piledriver in the Merseyside derby that crashed into the roof of Bruce Grobbelaar's net to put the Blues level at Anfield. Sheedy, along with Adrian Heath, then raised a pair of fingers in salute to the Kop. "I usually just put one finger up signalling a goal, but, it being the Kop end, two fingers automatically went up," he said later. "I got hauled up in front of the FA and I was like Ted Rogers trying to go from two fingers to one and trying to convince them it wasn't a V-sign."

— THE TOFFEES —

The sweets that spawned a thousand dodgy headlines

There is a certain amount of legend and myth surrounding the actual events that led to a black-and-white striped confectionery becoming synonymous with Everton Football Club and being responsible for a nickname, the Toffees, that has been a godsend to lazy headline writers for decades.

Two sweetshops are involved in this tale of candy-based rivalry, the first being *Ye Ancient Everton Toffee House*, owned by Old Ma Bushell and located near Anfield. They sold their Everton Toffee to the crowds on their way to watch the team play there and even earlier when the club was based at Priory Road and Stanley Park. However, when the move from Anfield to Goodison Park took place in 1892, Everton found themselves closer to another confectioner, Mother Noblett's Toffee Shop.

Spotting an opportunity, Mother Noblett's is said to have introduced a toffee with white sugar stripes and thus was born the Everton Mint that is still available today. However, Molly Bushell was not to be outdone, so the story goes, and pulled off a masterstroke by negotiating the right to sell her original Everton Toffee within Goodison Park itself. Her granddaughter Jemima Bushell wore her Sunday best and walked around the ground with a basket, selling toffees to the supporters – the modern day Toffee Lady mascot, a young lady in a blue and white dress who throws sweets to the crowd before every match, is said to be a nod to that tradition.

A slightly less intriguing take on the tale though is that Molly Bushell actually died in 1818, a long time before the football team was ever formed, and that the recipe for the Everton Toffee was simply sold to Mother Noblett's in 1894. They in turn introduced the white stripes and reinvented the sweet as the Everton Mint, still produced to this day by Barker and Dobson.

— TAXI! —

If any Everton manager hears the fans demanding that a taxi be called for him, he shouldn't take it as a sign of their helpfulness. "Taxi for (whoever)" has become shorthand for the sack, thanks to an incident that took place on 14th April 1961.

Johnny Carey, the ex-Manchester United player, had been appointed Everton manager in 1958 and with the benefit of chairman John Moores's financial backing brought stars to the club including Bobby Collins, Roy Vernon and Alex Young. Indeed, he led the Blues to their highest post-war league finish at the time, fifth, but Moores was not convinced that the Irishman had what it took to lead the club any further.

Both men attended a meeting of the FA together in London, with speculation rife that Harry Catterick, who had suddenly resigned as manager of Sheffield Wednesday, was being lined up for the Goodison hot seat. When Carey asked for assurances from Moores about his position, the Littlewoods chairman offered to discuss the matter in a taxi. By the time it arrived at their hotel, Carey was already the ex-manager of Everton Football Club.

— TROPHIES GALORE —

The Charity Shield played at Goodison on 16th August 1966 saw a remarkable array of silverware paraded on the pitch. Everton had the FA Cup, Liverpool brought the league trophy, and World Cup winners Ray Wilson and Roger Hunt carried out the Jules Rimet trophy

— THE BETTING SCANDAL OF 1964 —

Tony Kay, unfortunately, will not be remembered by the public at large as Britain's first £60,000 signing or for the fact that he was a talented midfielder who won the league with Everton in the 1962/63 season and a solitary England cap. The tenacious Yorkshireman would surely have added to that tally were it not for his involvement in a sordid affair that saw several players imprisoned and banned from professional football for life.

While playing for Sheffield Wednesday, the side who received the record fee for him in December 1962, Kay, along with teammates Peter Swann and David 'Bronco' Lane, were approached by Jimmy Gauld, once of Everton for a short spell, and, according to Kay, asked about a game that they might lose. None of the players fancied their chances away to Ipswich, and so they placed bets on the opposition. Sure enough, Wednesday did indeed go down 2–0 at Portman Road, although Kay himself received man-of-the-match awards in several newspapers.

In the middle of 1964 though, Gauld, a man with serious gambling problems and desperate for cash, sold his story to the *Sunday People*. He even recorded conversations with the players he had enticed to fix games and when the newspaper's evidence was passed on to the Director of Public Prosecutions, these tapes were used in court, one of the first times that that had happened in Britain. In the years to come, Kay found himself 'invited' to London to give the Kray twins an insight into an investigative technique that they clearly envisaged being utilised against themselves some day.

All four men, along with other professionals who had been corrupted by Gauld, received prison sentences. Kay's was for four months, although he eventually served ten weeks in an open prison near Leeds. Even more damaging though was the FA's life ban. It was later rescinded in 1974 but by that time it was too late for Kay who had seen a potentially glorious career robbed from him because of a single naive indiscretion.

"One of my happiest experiences was when I returned last year to Everton, to Goodison Park, for the club's centenary celebrations. I played 44 games for Everton when they won the league title, in

1962/63, and when I returned that day, walking out on to the pitch, I received an incredible ovation from the fans. The warmth of their reception meant everything to me, not least because I hadn't been back to Everton for years and yet they still remembered me. Do I regret placing that bet? Well, I think I was harshly punished. I won only £150 from the bet, but my whole career was destroyed. They took away the game I loved and I have never really recovered from that."

Tony Kay, speaking to *The Observer* in July 2004

— THE SHIRT OFF HIS BACK —

A bizarre incident in a league game at Highbury marked a low point in the career of Ghanaian international Alex Nyarko. The £4.5 million signing from Lens came to Everton with a glowing reputation – indeed he was reputed to be the new Patrick Vieira – but he failed to adjust to English football and a string of very poor performances culminated in the strange events of 21st April 2001.

With 70 minutes of the game gone and Everton trailing 3–1, one supporter decided he'd seen enough and wished to express his displeasure with what was on show. In particular he seemed unimpressed with Nyarko's input and so removed his own shirt, marched bare-chested across the pitch and offered to swap places with the bemused African.

Nyarko was shaken by the incident and demanded to be substituted, perhaps confirming suspicions that he wasn't the most wholehearted of competitors, and afterwards announced that he was so upset that he would be retiring from football, although he later changed his mind and said it was simply Everton he was unwilling to play for again.

Nyarko was subsequently loaned to AS Monaco and Paris Saint-Germain, although he did actually return to Goodison and play a further 11 games under David Moyes in the 2003/04 season.

"I'll need time to think about that. About five seconds."
Walter Smith, when asked about Nyarko's decision to retire.

— EVERTON LEGENDS: GRAEME SHARP —

Graeme Sharp: Only Dixie Dean has scored more Everton goals

Howard Kendall's team of the mid-1980s was the most successful in the club's history, so there are a lot of players from that side who could quite easily qualify for legendary status. One member though, Graeme Sharp, a £120,000 signing from Dumbarton in 1980, would eventually score more goals than any Everton player other than Dixie Dean, so it seems impossible to leave him out

Later in his ten-year Everton career he would develop into a traditional targetman, constantly looking for flick-ons and far post headers, but despite his height there was a lot more to his game than just aerial ability, especially in his early years. He was mobile, with a fierce shot, and scored a lot of memorable goals.

He struggled at first though, but then blossomed along with the rest of that wonderful team following the arrival of Andy Gray from Wolves in November 1983. Indeed, Sharp and Gray went on to form probably the most uncompromising front pairing the club has ever seen. They scored some crucial goals, too, including one each at Wembley in the 2–0 victory over Watford in the 1984 FA Cup Final.

Sharp also scored the equaliser in the titanic European Cup Winners' Cup semi-final against Bayern Munich the following season, as well as 21 goals in the league, as Everton raced to their first championship in 15 years. One in particular stands out just a little bit more than the rest though.

Everton had not won at Anfield since 1970 when they made their way across the park on 20th October 1984, so when Sharp controlled Gary Stevens' long ball with his left foot, before volleying it with his right from 25 yards and leaving Bruce Grobelaar grasping at thin air, it was a momentous occasion to say the least. The game finished 1–0 and the whole of football began to sit up and take Everton's young team very seriously indeed. The strike itself won *Match of the Day*'s Goal of the Season and is arguably the most memorable effort by any Everton player in living memory. The reaction of the Everton fans who invaded the pitch to mob Sharp is almost as legendary too, especially the ecstatic celebrations of the Blue with the flailing arms who earned himself the nickname of the Windmill.

Sharp won another league champions' medal in 1986/87 before leaving for Oldham Athletic who he would serve both as a player and then manager until 1997. Always an extremely popular and approachable figure, he's now back at Everton working as Charities' Manager as well as a pundit for local radio.

Graeme Sharp factfile
Born: Glasgow, 16th October 1960
Appearances: 426 (21 as substitute)
Goals: 159 goals
Other clubs: Dumbarton, Oldham Athletic
Full international appearances while at Everton: 12 for Scotland

— OUT OF THE BLUE —

Much as Evertonians would like to believe that every player lucky enough to pull on the royal blue has had star quality, the fact is that not everyone can be an Alex Young or a Dixie Dean. Still, of all the duffers that the Blues have signed down the years, few players have been so maligned as Bernie Wright. Ironically nicknamed Bernie the Bolt, after a character on the television show *The Golden Shot,* the hirsute Wright struck a menacing figure. However, despite impressing Harry Catterick when facing Everton for Walsall in an FA Cup tie in January 1972, the Birmingham-born striker hardly struck fear into opposing defences. Indeed, his performances in his 11 appearances for Everton provoked nothing but mirth amongst the fans. His somewhat Neanderthal image was only reinforced when he shrugged off a kick in the head from Sheffield United's Eddie Colqhoun, only for the centre half – hardly a shrinking violet himself – to be taken off with a broken toe.

In fairness to Wright though, it wasn't his fault he had been promoted to a level beyond his abilities, and although Everton sold him back to Walsall after just one year he went on to enjoy a good career in the lower leagues with the Saddlers and Port Vale.

— WHY DON'T YOU? —

Some of the extra-curricular interests of Everton players and staff down the years:

Willie Donachie	Sketching portraits
Mick Bernard	Speedway
Duncan Ferguson	Pigeon racing
Brian Labone	Stamp collecting
Martin Dobson	Gardening
Dixie Dean	Greyhound racing
George Wood	Ornithology
Mike Pejic	Farming

— SHINE A LIGHT —

The first match played under floodlights at Goodison Park was a friendly against Liverpool on 9th October 1957. Everton won 2–0, with two goals from Eddie Thomas. Ever the imitators, the Reds had their own lights switched on three weeks later and a second leg was played to mark the occasion. Liverpool triumphed 3–2 on that occasion.

Everton's first league match under the lights was on 17th October 1957 when they drew 2–2 with Arsenal.

— THE PEOPLE'S CLUB —

Only days after the sacking of Walter Smith, David Moyes was unveiled as the Everton manager on 14th March 2002. These press conferences are often much of a muchness, with new bosses talking about the excitement of the challenge ahead, etc. but Moyes was to make a statement – completely unrehearsed and off the cuff according to a later interview with Everton's Head of Public Relations, Ian Ross – that stood out and struck a chord with Evertonians (and a very raw nerve with Liverpudlians, as it happens): "I am from a city (Glasgow) that is not unlike Liverpool. I am joining the people's club. The majority of people you meet on the street are Everton fans. It is a fantastic opportunity, something you dream about."

The People's Club tag certainly stuck, immediately inspiring all manner of T-shirts, banners and chants. The club themselves have adopted it and include it in much of their branding and merchandising. Indeed, some people even say they are getting a bit sick of it now.

— MAYBE THIS YEAR —

Twice finalists, in 1977 and 1984, and semi-finalists in 1988 and 2008, the League Cup in all its many incarnations is the one domestic honour that still eludes Everton.

— ILLEGAL ALIEN —

On 28th August 1999, Everton played Derby County and lost 1–0 thanks to a 47th-minute goal by the Rams' Argentine import, Esteban Fuertes. Fast forward to November of that same year, as Jim Smith's side returned from a trip to Portugal, and customs officials discover that the £2 million striker is travelling with a forged passport. He's not allowed to return to the UK but the one goal he scored during his short career in the Midlands is allowed to stand.

— SPOT ON —

Fans of almost all clubs will tell you that they dread their side settling games in penalty shoot-outs. Evertonians are no different, although with a record of six lost and only three won, perhaps Toffees might have more reason than most to look away when their players line up from 12 yards.

And it all started so well, with a thrilling triumph over Borussia Mönchengladbach on 4th November 1970. A 1–1 draw in the first leg of this European Cup second-round match was followed by one of the all time thrillers at Goodison in the return. Johnny Morrisey opened the scoring in the first minute, only for Laumann to equalise and set up the shoot-out. Joe Royle missed the opening kick for the Blues, but a miss by Laumann and then a tremendous Andy Rankin save from Muller saw the Toffees through.

However, Everton lost the next four shoot-outs they were involved in, only triumphing again when the much maligned Richard Wright kept out three Newcastle kicks in a League Cup third round tie at St James' Park on 6th November 2002.

Since then, though, Everton have only won another one, at Ashton Gate in the League Cup, and then lost one at the Riverside in the same competition. Quite sickeningly, they also lost the shoot-out in the home game against Fiorentina in the last 16 of the UEFA Cup in 2008. That heartbreaking defeat came after heroically clawing back a two-goal deficit incurred in the first leg in Italy.

— THIS IS ENGLAND —

Forget the Mighty Magyars of 1953, the first side other than one of the Home Nations to record a victory on English soil were the Republic of Ireland, at Goodison Park. The game took place on 21st September 1949 and the visitors added insult to English injury by fielding something of a cobbled together side, minus several key players, including Everton's own Tommy Eglington who missed out through injury.

Pat Corr and Peter Farrell did turn out in green shirts on their own turf though, and the latter sealed a 2–0 win with a goal at the Gwladys Street end after Aston Villa's Con Martin had put the Irish ahead with a penalty.

— PASS THE SOAP —

Premier League games in which two Everton players have been sent for an early bath:

Date	Result	Players dismissed
28th Dec 1992	QPR 4 Everton 2	Neville Southall and Paul Rideout
1st Feb 1995	Newcastle 2 Everton 0	Earl Barret and Barry Horne
4th March 1995	Leicester 2 Everton 2	Vinny Samways and Duncan Ferguson
8th May 2000	Leeds 1 Everton 1	Richard Dunne and Don Hutchison
19th April 2003	Everton 1 Liverpool 2	David Weir and Gary Naysmith
28th Dec 2005	Everton 1 Liverpool 3	Phil Neville and Mikel Arteta

— EVERTON LEGENDS: ALEX YOUNG —

Alex Young: the Golden Vision

Alex Young was the man they called the Golden Vision. Indeed, mention his name to anyone who followed the Blues in the 1960s and then watch them get all misty-eyed over a slight and skilful forward who embodied the School of Science method of playing the game.

Already a Scottish international, and the winner of two league titles north of the border when Everton paid £55,000 to prise him and full back George Thomson from Heart of Midlothian, Young's capture was considered something of a gamble when he arrived in November 1960. Indeed, he was injured when he arrived at Goodison and didn't score a league goal until March 1961. Johnny Carey infamously took his taxi ride the following month and Young was later to express regret at not being fit enough to score the goals that could have kept the manager in a job. It was a knee injury that hampered the start of his Everton career, although a more unusual ailment was the curse he had to endure throughout his playing days. Young suffered terribly with blisters on his feet, earning him an alternative nickname, the rather less complimentary Tenderfoot.

Under Harry Catterick though, Young struck up a deadly partnership with Roy Vernon, whose pace and eye for goal complemented the Scotsman's vision and deftness of touch. His 22 goals in the 1962/63 season, particularly the single strike that separated Everton and closest rivals Tottenham on 20th April 1963, were instrumental in bringing the league title back to Goodison for the first time since the Second World War.

Evertonians idolised the blond-haired Scot by this point and according to Steve Johnson, of the superb **evertonresults.com**, "This was hero worship the like of which no other Everton player has since come close to receiving. Think of how loved the two Duncans – McKenzie and Ferguson – were, and multiply that by a very large number indeed and you'd still be way out."

The idolisation of Young was such that fans staged protests when he was dropped for Fred Pickering in March 1964. Even more infamously, Harry Catterick was jostled to the floor after a defeat at Bloomfield Road in January 1966 when the 16-year-old debutant Joe Royle took Young's place.

Later in that same season though, he would be back in the team – indeed the outcry was about the dropping of Pickering for Mike Trebilcock – and although he didn't score Young played his part in the famous FA Cup Final win over Sheffield Wednesday.

In 1968, the year that Young was sold to Irish side Glentoran for £10,000, Ken Loach directed a television play about working-class Scousers, centred on a family of Evertonians, and in some ways this helped to immortalise Young by being titled *The Golden Vision* after his nickname.

Alex Young factfile
Born: Loanhead, 3rd February 1937
Appearances: 272 (3 as substitute)
Goals: 89
Other clubs: Heart of Midlothian, Glentoran, Stockport County
Full international appearances while at Everton: 2 for Scotland

— STARS OF THE SILVER SCREEN —

World Cup-winning left back Ray Wilson's first name was short for Ramon, not Raymond. He was apparently named after the Mexican matinee idol Ramón Novarro. Likewise, a somewhat less celebrated full back, Mitch Ward, was christened Mitchum, after Robert, the stone-faced star of *The Sundowners*. Jack Cock, who played for the Blues in the 1920s, even appeared in a couple of films, *The Winning Goal* and *The Great Game*. The latter marked the first screen performance of a young Rex Harrison, no less.

— COLOUR ME BAD —

The first FA Cup Final to be televised in colour was the 1968 encounter between West Bromwich Albion and clear favourites Everton. Two other milestones were also set in same match. Dennis Clarke became the first substitute used in a final, when he replaced John Kaye for Albion, and Jeff Astle became the first man since Jackie Milburn in 1951 to score in every round of the competition – his strike in extra time winning the Cup for the Baggies.

— DOWN BUT NOT OUT —

Manchester United's Kevin Moran became the first player ever sent off in an FA Cup Final, for his foul on Peter Reid in 1985. Everton couldn't take advantage though, despite their numerical superiority, and Norman Whiteside's extra-time curler beat Neville Southall, preventing the league champions from completing a treble. Indeed, almost all Evertonians believe that the exertions of winning the Cup Winners' Cup in midweek took their toll on the Toffees at a humid Wembley in something of a subdued match.

"Given another day we would have beaten United easily. We'd beaten them in the league but we were just exhausted at Wembley, mentally and physically. After 20 minutes you just started to feel heavy-legged and it got the better of you."
Graeme Sharp

— THE INFRINGEMENT —

It wouldn't surprise Evertonians if Treorchy-born referee Clive Thomas ended up showing people his birth certificate in later life, to prove that he wasn't actually christened 'that c*** Clive Thomas'.

Now there has been more than the odd injustice inflicted on the Toffees down the years, but in truth the events of the 1977 FA Cup semi-final represent the mother lode. The Blues faced Liverpool at Maine Road on 23rd April, only ten days after losing the second replay of the League Cup Final to Aston Villa. Everton's derby record going into the match was grim – they'd scored only one goal against the old enemy since their last victory over five years ago. In the dying moments of a game finely poised at 2–2, thanks to equalisers from Duncan McKenzie and Bruce Rioch, Ronnie Goodlass swung a cross into the Liverpool box. Substitute Bryan Hamilton gambled on a run towards the near post and managed to divert the ball past Ray Clemence with his midriff. There was no time for Liverpool to even think about an equaliser of their own; Wembley beckoned for the Blues. But no.

Thomas disallowed the goal and later commented that Hamilton was close to tears as he implored him to let it stand. For his part, the referee refused to give an adequate explanation for his actions. He wavered between the enigmatic 'infringement of the laws of the Football Association' and the more specific offside – although the linesman hadn't flagged and Hamilton was clearly onside – and then insisted that Hamilton *must have* handled. He hadn't.

Everyone knew deep down that Everton's chance had gone then, and true to form Liverpool won the replay 3–0. To this day there is a generation of Evertonians still scarred by the memories of what Thomas did that afternoon.

"We probably hated him more than the fans. He blatantly stole results from us on more than one occasion."
Bob Latchford

— THE PRINCE OF WALES —

If Dixie Dean says that you are the best player he ever saw then it's fair to say that you must be a bit special. And the great Everton number 9 made just that declaration about Tommy 'TG' Jones, the tall Welshman who played centre half for the Blues from 1936 to 1950.

Another great Everton centre forward, Tommy Lawton, also rated Jones highly and bemoaned the fact that he was marked by his club team-mate when he made his own England debut against Wales. Lawton did score one of England's goals in a 4–2 defeat, but it was a penalty and he declared afterwards that thanks to Jones's defensive skills, "It was the only shot I had in the whole game."

Jones won a league title with the Toffees in 1939 but then the Second World War intervened. In one of the less glorious chapters in the club's history, Jones fell out with the Everton board after the war and his appearances were limited. He asked for a transfer – indeed in 1948 AS Roma were willing to pay £15,500 to take him to Italy – but his requests were repeatedly turned down and his career at Everton petered out.

He later became manager of Bangor City, and in 1962 they drew Napoli in the preliminary round of the European Cup Winners' Cup. With no away goals ruling then – if there had been then Jones' men would have gone through – it took a play-off at Highbury, after the aggregate from the home and away legs finished 3–3, for the Italians to triumph over the non-league Welshmen.

"Tommy had everything. No coach could ever coach him or teach him anything. He was neater than John Charles, for instance, and could get himself out of trouble just by running towards the ball and then letting it run between his legs, knowing his team-mate would be in a position to make it."
Dixie Dean

"He had the great capacity to stroke the ball and the best right foot in the business. He was never satisfied with his performance and always drove sides on. He was calm in a crisis and both delicate and sophisticated on the ground."
Tommy Lawton

— 'I RAN FROM IRAN' —

Alan Whittle is credited with scoring the goals during the tail end of the 1969/70 season that pushed Everton over the finish line and clinched the league title. His six goals in six games were certainly crucial – not least the winners in tight matches at Stoke City and Tottenham.

He left Everton for Crystal Palace in December 1972, though, and eventually ended up, of all places, in Iran. After struggling at Leyton Orient he was given the chance in 1977 to join Persopolis, the Iranian version of Manchester United according to Whittle, and despite the cultural differences he settled in to a great lifestyle. He said, "I could have anything I liked. Food, booze, cars . . . absolutely anything. The Shah had it right because it was very westernised."

Seventeen months later, the Ayatollah Khomeini overthrew the Shah and Whittle was forced to flee the country, leaving his booze, cars and thousands of pounds behind him.

— LEITCH'S LEGACY —

Goodison Park's principle designer was the Scot, Archibald Leitch, whose trademark criss-cross balustrades are still visible to this day along the Bullens Road side of the ground. He was initially a designer of factories in his home city of Glasgow, before being commissioned to work on Ibrox Park in 1899. Despite the fact that 26 people were killed in a crush at that ground in 1902, Leitch's reputation remained intact and he went on to work on Old Trafford, Maine Road, Anfield, Villa Park, Hampden, Ayresome Park, Stamford Bridge, Highbury, Twickenham and many other famous British sporting venues.

Apart from Goodison, Leitch designs that can still be seen today include the Johnny Haynes Stand at Craven Cottage and the facade of the Main Stand at Ibrox, both of which are listed buildings.

— EVERTON LEGENDS:
HOWARD KENDALL (PLAYER) —

What would Everton's history be without the man born in Ryton-on-Tyne on the 22nd May 1946? Considerably poorer, that's for sure, because not only did the elegant midfielder Howard Kendall form part of the legendary 'Holy Trinity', alongside Colin Harvey and Alan Ball at the heart of the team of the late 1960s, but he also went on to become the most successful manager in the club's history.

Already a schoolboy international – he went on to captain England to victory in the Little World Cup in 1964 – Kendall signed as an apprentice with Preston North End in June 1961. His appearance at Wembley 1964 FA Cup Final made him the youngest player to have graced that stage of the competition since 1879 and it wasn't long before the top clubs began to take an interest in such a prodigious talent. It was actually believed that he was bound for Anfield of all places until Harry Catterick stole a march on Bill Shankly and fatefully signed Kendall for £80,000 in the March of 1967.

A great passer of the ball with a lovely technique when volleying, his economical style perfectly complemented the industry of Ball and the mazy dribbling of Harvey, the man who would become his trusted right-hand man in years to come. He was instrumental in the championship win in 1969/70 and yet famously never won a full England cap – many rate him as the best English player to have been completely overlooked, especially when you consider that even John Fashanu has two caps to his name.

Kendall captained the Blues from 1970 to 1974 when he was part of the deal, along with Archie Styles, that brought Bob Latchford to Goodison Park. Everton fans were disappointed to see such a class act leave though, but it was at St Andrews, encouraged by manager Freddie Goodwin, where he would make the first foray into coaching that would eventually bring him back to Everton (see *Everton Legends: Howard Kendall (Manager)*, page 85).

Howard Kendall factfile
Born: Ryton-on-Tyne, 22nd May 1946
Appearances: 274 (3 as substitute)
Goals: 30
Other clubs: Preston North End, Birmingham City, Stoke City,
Blackburn Rovers
Full international appearances while at Everton: 0

— BROTHER BEYOND —

Some Everton players with brothers who also played professional
football:

Wayne Clarke	Allan (Leeds United)
Phil Jagielka	Steve (Shrewsbury Town)
Phil Neville	Gary (Manchester United)
Jack Sharp	Bert (Everton)
Dave Watson	Alex (Liverpool)
Joleon Lescott	Aaron (Bristol Rovers
Bob Latchford	Dave (Birmingham City)
	and Peter (West Bromwich Albion)
Ian Snodin	Glynn (Leeds United)
Billy Scott	Elisha (Liverpool)
Walter Balmer	Robert (Everton)
Mike Pejic	Mel (Stoke City)

— TELLING PORKIES —

The name Everton is of Old English origin and means, roughly,
boar settlement. Clearly the possibility for bad jokes there is
endless. As well as the Everton in Liverpool, there are others in
Britain (in Bedfordshire, Hampshire, Nottinghamshire and
Shetland), the United States (in Arkansas, Indiana and Missouri),
Australia and even South Africa (near Durban).

— THE TURNSTILE FRAUD OF 1895 —

Although today's tabloid press have developed football scandals into daily fare for the nation's breakfast tables, shadiness and impropriety are hardly new phenomena. In 1895, Everton officials became suspicious that the takings from home gates seemed low, although they tallied perfectly well with the numbers on the turnstiles. Further investigation, with plain-clothes officers observing the gates, showed that a number of the counters on the turnstiles had been turned back 200 units. This allowed some unscrupulous gatemen to pocket £5 and the figures would still tally.

Eventually a widespread fraud was uncovered and 15 arrests were made, including the groundsman and the mechanic who maintained the turnstiles.

— LEAPS AND BOUNDS —

Some branded him a great entertainer, others a fair-weather player, but Duncan McKenzie's two seasons at Goodison in the late 1970s saw him score a healthy 21 goals in 61 starts. Whenever his name is mentioned though, the first thing people say is "He could jump over a Mini and throw a golf ball the length of the pitch."

Admittedly not the most useful skills for a footballer.

— BY ROYAL APPROVAL —

Goodison Park became the first Football League ground to be visited by a ruling monarch when King George V and Queen Mary were guests of the club on 11th July 1913.

— THE SCHOOL OF SCIENCE —

"Everton always manage to serve up football of the highest scientific order."
Steve Bloomer, England international 1895–1907

— OWZAT! —

Jack Sharp is most well known to fashion-conscious men of a certain age who remember frequenting the Liverpool sport shop that bore his name, looking for the latest Adidas trainers (or trainees, to use the proper local vernacular). He was one of Everton's stars at the turn of the century though, after signing from Aston Villa in 1899, and he went on to score 80 goals in 342 appearances. His sporting prowess wasn't confined to the football field either. As well as winning two caps for England at soccer, he also played three cricket Tests for his country and scored a century against Australia at The Oval in 1909.

His brother Bert, while not quite as accomplished as Jack, was a good all-rounder too, appearing ten times for Everton and playing county cricket for Herefordshire.

— HAT-TRICK HEROES —

The top hat trick scorers for the Toffees in all competitions:

Dixie Dean	37
Bobby Parker	7
Tony Cottee	6
Bert Freeman	6
Alex Latta	6
Bob Latchford	5
Jack Southworth	5
Alex 'Sandy' Young	5
John Willie Parker	4
Graeme Sharp	4
Eddie Wainwright	4

— THE DIXIE DEAN OF THE STIFFS —

When he made the step up to the big time, the ex-butcher's boy Stuart Barlow cruelly earned the nickname Jigsaw, because of his propensity to fall apart in the box. It was a different story for him in the reserves, where between 1990 and 1996 he bagged 84 goals.

— TO THE TOWER —

Everton's rather distinctive badge features a tower flanked by two wreaths and the club's motto *Nil satis nisi optimum*, meaning roughly 'Nothing but the best is good enough'.

While the club itself has been around for well over a century, the badge's history doesn't go back quite as far. Indeed, it was designed just before the Second World War by Theo Kelly, the club secretary who would later become manager. It was in fact for a club necktie that Kelly originally came up with the crest – the badge wasn't actually incorporated into the design of the kit until as late as 1980.

The inclusion of the wreaths was straightforward enough – they are simply a heraldic symbol that represents winners. The tower though is more specific to the club, as it is a representation of Prince Rupert's Tower, a bridewell – essentially a small jail – built in 1787 and located on Netherfield Road, a short distance from Goodison Park.

— EVERTON LEGENDS: ALAN BALL —

Alan Ball; Mr Perpetual Motion

After starring in England's World Cup-winning team, Alan Ball was more or less the hottest property in English football in the summer of 1966. Diminutive in stature, Ball had been rejected by the likes of Wolverhampton Wanderers and Bolton as a schoolboy because of his slight frame. Those setbacks only made him more fiercely determined to succeed, though, and encouraged and cajoled by his father, Alan Sr, he turned professional with Blackpool in 1962. Taking the place of the legendary Stanley Matthews, he made his professional debut in a 2–1 win at Anfield and a star was born. He received the first of his 72 England caps in 1964, then came the World Cup and a British-record £110,000 move to Harry Catterick's Everton, despite the attentions of Don Revie and Leeds United who were desperate to add such a fierce competitor to their side.

Ball scored on his league debut for the Toffees, the only goal at Craven Cottage on the opening day of the 1966/67 season, and went on to form the third part of the famous 'Holy Trinity', alongside Howard Kendall and Colin Harvey. Indeed, Kendall said of him, "We arrived at Everton in the same season and hit it off immediately. He was such a bubbly character, it was really Alan who made the partnership with me and Colin work as well as it did. He was undoubtedly the best player I ever played with."

His competitive streak often boiled over though and while idolised by the Goodison crowd – not least when he scored twice in a 3–2 win over Liverpool – and respected for his ability by his team-mates, his abrasive attitude often caused conflict within the dressing room. Dubbed Mr Perpetual Motion for his energy and enthusiasm, his contribution to the Everton cause was massive, not least for the 79 goals he scored from midfield in the five and a half seasons he spent in royal blue.

Ball apparently tossed his FA Cup runners-up medal to the floor in disgust at Wembley in 1968, but went on to add a league title to his World Cup winner's medal in 1970. However, as Evertonians settled in and awaited a period of dominance after being crowned champions, their form slipped mysteriously and, most shocking of all, Catterick sold Ball to Arsenal for £220,000 in December 1971. Some Evertonians who remember that era still haven't recovered to this day.

While Ball went on to serve Arsenal well for five years he never won another domestic honour and sadly his reputation was perhaps sullied in the eyes of the nation at large because of his rather undistinguished managerial career at the likes of Stoke City, Southampton, Portsmouth and Manchester City. Evertonians, though, will always remember the little ginger-haired bundle of energy who wore white boots and perhaps tried to live by the club's motto, of never being satisfied by anything but the best, more than anyone else who ever pulled on an Everton jersey.

Many of the grown men who were left shaken by his transfer in 1971 were then moved to tears when Ball sadly died unexpectedly in April 2007.

"It was just Disneyland. Fantastic. It was everything you wanted to do in your life. Go on a Saturday and be dead confident in front of thousands of people – no, millions of people because television had just started then. I had the most incredible years, just training, laughing, playing football, then getting paid at the end of the week, and getting paid more if you won – come on!" **Alan Ball**

> **Alan Ball factfile**
> Born: Farnworth, 12th May 1945
> Died: 25th April 2007
> Appearances: 251
> Goals: 79
> Other clubs: Blackpool, Arsenal, Southampton, Philadelphia Fury, Vancouver Whitecaps, Eastern Athletic, Bristol Rovers
> Full international appearances while at Everton: 39 for England

— YOUNG GUN —

At 16 years and 271 days, James Vaughan became Everton's youngest ever first-team player when he made his debut as a late substitute against Crystal Palace on 10th April 2005. When sliding home Kevin Kilbane's cross in the dying minutes he also became the Premiership's youngest ever scorer, a record previously held by Leeds's James Milner and before him Everton's own Wayne Rooney.

— ANYBODY HOME? —

Everton have the rather dubious distinction of playing in front of the top flight's lowest post-war attendance when they visited Selhurst Park to face Wimbledon on 26th January 1993. Only 3,039 people bothered to watch Everton win 3–1 thanks to a brace from Tony Cottee and a rare Ian Snodin effort.

— CLASSIC MATCHES: EVERTON 3 SHEFFIELD WEDNESDAY 2, 1966 —

To most football fans, Wembley 1966 is all about Geoff Hurst and a 'Russian' linesman. For Evertonians, though, the abiding memories from the Twin Towers that summer concern a little known Cornishman and the greatest comeback ever in an FA Cup Final.

Harry Catterick had proven on many occasions that he was never one to shy away from unpopular decisions and his omission of Fred Pickering for the trip to Wembley, where the Blues would face the manager's old club, Sheffield Wednesday, caused consternation amongst the Everton followers. In Pickering's stead, playing up front alongside Alex Young was Mike Trebilcock, a 21-year-old with only eight senior appearances to his name. Indeed, he would only go on to make another six after the final before transferring to Portsmouth in January 1968.

Everton came into the match as the first side ever to make it to the final without conceding a goal, but any hopes of maintaining that stingy defensive record were wiped out when Jim McCalliog's shot deflected home off Ray Wilson after only four minutes. Alex Young saw what looked like a good goal disallowed for offside before a big appeal for a penalty was turned down when Ron Springett in the Wednesday goal appeared to bring the Golden Vision down. And on 57 minutes things looked even worse for the Blues when David Ford doubled the Yorkshire club's lead.

That goal simply set the scene for the comeback, though, started two minutes later when Trebilcock pulled one back for the Toffees. Another five minutes later and the game was all square. Brian Labone headed a deep free kick back to the edge of the Wednesday area and Trebilcock was the quickest to react, flashing a low shot through a crowd of defenders and into the bottom corner of Springett's goal.

A shell-shocked Wednesday never recovered and Everton completed the stunning turnaround with the killer goal on 74 minutes. A slight mis-control by stalwart defender Gerry Young allowed Derek Temple a run on goal. He raced clear and struck the most clinical of finishes, angling his shot across Springett and watching in delight as it nestled in the back of the net. Unlike another effort at that same end in a few months time, no one was in any doubt that this had crossed the line when the final whistle blew and captain Labone climbed the stairs to receive the cup from Princess Margaret.

—THE THINGS THEY SAID —

"Everton are really missing Arteta, and it's sticking out like a sore throat."
Former Evertonian **Ronnie Goodlass**

"I thought 'What is more uniquely Scouse than anything?' and I thought of Everton. To me Liverpool was more McDonald's but you can't have one without the other."
Lee Mavers of the La's

"Howard said 'Right, no training Monday. Just report to Mr Lau's in Southport at 12 o'clock.' It would be totally taboo now that you would have a Chinese meal and drink until the early hours but that was his way of good team bonding and it was good. There were some good afternoons enjoyed by everybody."
Paul Power on Howard Kendall's old-school management style

"With Manchester City it was a love affair, but with Everton it's more like a marriage."
Howard Kendall

"Everton are a bigger club than Liverpool. Everywhere you go on Merseyside you bump into Everton supporters."
Graeme Souness -Yes, *that* Graeme Souness

"Football was never the same for me after I left Everton and although I always wanted to win, losing never really seemed to hurt any more."
Kevin Ratcliffe

"Lloyd McGrath is lucky he's not running in a gelding plate now. That tackle was so high it was very nearly a squeaky-voice job."

John Sillett, Coventry manager, objecting to a challenge by Dave Watson

"Harry Catterick never got involved: he left it to the trainers. You never saw Harry with a tracksuit on but all of a sudden he'd come out with one on and we'd be saying, 'Who's coming, who's coming?' Then John Moores turned up and he's saying, 'Hello Mr Moores!' and he's running about in a tracksuit and all that."
Gordon West

"Merseyside derbies usually last 90 minutes and I'm sure today's won't be any different."
Trevor Brooking

"It was that game that put the Everton ship back on the road."
Alan Green

— THE FIRST MATCH —

Played at Anfield on 8th September 1888, Everton's first ever game in the Football League saw them play hosts to Accrington. Over 10,000 supporters turned out and saw Everton triumph 2–1, thanks to a brace from George Fleming. The Everton line-up on that historic occasion was:

Robert Smalley
Nick Ross
Alec Dick
George Dobson
Robert S Jones
Johnny Holt
George Farmer
Edgar Chadwick
David Waugh
George Fleming
William Lewis

— GIANT-KILLERS, THE TABLES TURNED —

As the club with more years in the top flight of English football than any other, Everton have thankfully had few opportunities to be considered giant-killers. However, the Blues have spent a total of four seasons outside the top flight and did overcome First Division opposition in the cup competitions during those brief periods, so strictly speaking the following results do class as giant killings:

Date	Competition	Result
14th Feb 1931	FA Cup rd 4	Everton 5
		Grimsby Town 3
14th Feb 1953	FA Cup rd 5	Everton 2
		Manchester United 1
28th Feb 1953	FA Cup rd 6	Aston Villa 0 Everton 1

— OUT OF AFRICA —

Everton have made a number of high-profile signings of African players since the mid-1990s, including the Nigerians Daniel Amokachi, Joseph Yobo and Ayegbeni Yakubu. The links go back a lot further than that, though, to the first overseas player to represent the club, David James Murray, who signed from Wynberg, South Africa in August 1925. He scored on his debut against Cardiff City but only played three games before moving to Bristol City.

— GO JINGLE JANGLE —

Incredibly, given the length of time that both clubs have been in the top flight, Vinny Samways and Simon Davies are the only players Everton have ever bought from Tottenham Hotspur. Anyone who ever saw the pair of them play for Everton might suggest that it would be best if they don't bother buying more off them either.

— EVERTON LEGENDS: NEVILLE SOUTHALL —

Big Nev: 751 games for Everton

It's a rare privilege to be able to watch at work an individual who is the very best at what they do and, arguably, may even be the best there has ever been. In the world. You will struggle to find may Evertonians though who will tell you that there's ever been a better goalkeeper than Neville Southall, the crumpled Welshman who appeared an incredible 751 times for the Blues – the club record by an enormous margin.

Anything but conventional throughout his career, few people would have guessed that the former hod-carrier and binman was destined for greatness as he did the rounds of Welsh non-league clubs before Bury eventually took him on as a professional at the relatively advanced age of 21. He caught Howard Kendall's eye and moved to Goodison for £150,000 in 1981, as one of the Magnificent Seven, and initially he looked to have about as much future as Mike Walsh and Alan Biley as he competed with Jim Arnold for the number 1 shirt. He was even sent out on loan to Port Vale for a short spell at the start of 1983. A fanatical trainer and obsessively driven, Southall never let these initial setbacks deter him though, and by the end of 1983 he was firmly ensconced as first-choice keeper, a position that he would hold for the next 15 years.

He was as influential as any other player as the fortunes of Howard Kendall's side turned around and stormed to victory in the 1984 FA Cup before enjoying league and European glory the following season. Indeed, Southall's most famous save was key to Everton being crowned champions in 1984/85. On 3rd April 1985, with the Blues 2–1 up against a Spurs side who were only three points behind in the table, the game was entering the final minutes when Southall jack-knifed in mid-air and pushed Marc Falco's bullet header over the bar, to the astonishment of everyone inside White Hart Lane.

His heroics earned him the Football Writers' Association Footballer of the Year award and the widely held belief – amongst Evertonians at least – is that his absence during the end of the 1985/86 season, with an ankle injury picked up on a disgraceful pitch at Landsdowne Road while playing for Wales, was key to the Blues narrowly missing out on a league and FA Cup double to Liverpool.

Unlike some of the other stars, Southall stuck around and endured the club's slow decline as the 1980s became the 1990s. At one point he looked so upset though that he even staged a bizarre half-time protest, sitting in his goalmouth on the opening day of the 1990/91 season after visitors Leeds had gone 3–0 up before the break. Still, despite those lows he enjoyed a last hurrah at Wembley in 1995, rolling back the years to at times contemptuously deny Alex Ferguson's men an equaliser in the FA Cup Final.

Southall finally left Everton for Stoke in February 1998 and then spent something of a nomadic existence, turning out for the likes of Torquay, Huddersfield, Rhyl and York, and then briefly managing Hastings. It always looked as though his outspokenness and unconventional demeanour would hamper him when it came to pursuing a career in management though, and that has unfortunately proven the case. However, his surliness and eccentricity are attributes that only endear Evertonians even more to the colossus they know simply as Big Nev.

Neville Southall factfile
Born: Llandudno, 16th September 1958
Appearances: 751
Goals: 0
Other clubs: Conwy United, Bangor City, Winsford United, Bury, Port Vale, Southend United, Stoke City, Doncaster Rovers, Torquay United, Bradford City, Huddersfield, Rhyl, York City.
Full international appearances while at Everton: 92 for Wales

— FIRST OF MANY, HOPEFULLY —

The first Everton player to score at the new Wembley Stadium was Jack Rodwell, grabbing the only goal in the England under-16s win over Spain on 28th April 2007.

— ON THE FIDDLE —

No, not the infamous turnstile scandal of 1895. This fiddle belongs to an Everton record holder, one Jack Southworth, the Blackburn-born centre forward who enjoyed an illustrious career with his home-town club before he was sold to Everton for £400 in 1893. Unfortunately, the crowd favourite spent only a little over one season with the Toffees before he was forced to retire through injury. In that time though, he managed to capture two club records. First, he scored six goals in one match, in a 7–1 defeat of West Bromwich Albion on 30th December 1893. Also, the 36 goals he scored in only 32 games for Everton represents, unsurprisingly, the club's best ever goals-to-game ratio.

Oh, the fiddle. On retirement, Southworth dedicated himself to music as keenly as he had to the art of scoring goals, going on to become a violinist with Manchester's famous Hallé Orchestra.

— CLASSIC MATCHES:
EVERTON 4 LIVERPOOL 4, 1991 —

This, possibly the most memorable derby game ever, took place on 20th February 1991. There should have been no need for this FA Cup fifth round replay at Goodison, as Everton had been denied the most clear-cut penalty imaginable in the initial tie at Anfield. Referee Neil Midgely ludicrously accused Pat Nevin of diving following a blatant trip by Gary Ablett, so the game finished scoreless and the scene was set for a night of incredible drama.

Peter Beardsley scored in the first half for Liverpool, only for Graeme Sharp to equalise shortly after the break. Beardsley, who would later weave his magic in a blue shirt, put the Reds back in front on 71 minutes with a powerful drive, only for a mix-up between Steve Nicol and Bruce Grobbelaar to allow Sharp to slide in and level matters again almost immediately. At 77 minutes, Liverpool scored again, this time through Ian Rush, and as time ticked away it looked as if they had finally done enough to progress to the next round of the cup. However, Tony Cottee, who had been out of favour with Howard Kendall, was introduced for the last five minutes, and with less than 60 seconds left on the clock and the whistles of the Kopites ringing out, the ex-West Ham man slotted coolly past Grobbelaar to force extra time.

The crowd were almost as exhausted as the players by this point but the action was far from over. Southall kept the visitors at bay until just before the end of the first period of extra time, when John Barnes scored one of the most memorable derby goals, curling a long range effort into the top corner. Remarkably, though, the Toffees still weren't beaten. When Glenn Hysen – don't let Kopites try and convince you that they've never bought any real dogs – put a back pass through Grobbelaar's legs, Cottee was again on hand to force home Everton's fourth equaliser of the night.

A week later, by which time Kenny Dalglish had shocked football by resigning from his position as manager of Liverpool, Dave Watson's goal in the second replay, again at Goodison, was enough to end the saga. For all the good it did, as the Blues were beaten 2–1 at West Ham in the next round.

— TOP OF THE CHARTS, ONCE (PRE-WAR) —

Players who topped the Everton goalscoring charts for only one season:

Edgar Chadwick, 1888/89 – 6 goals
One of the most renowned players of the day, he played in Everton's first ever league match against Accrington and was an ever-present in the first title-winning team. He also represented England on seven occasions and in his later career went on to manage the Dutch national team between 1908 and 1913.

Alex Latta, 1891/92 – 17 goals
A tricky winger signed from Dumbarton Athletic, he was one of the stars of the 1890/91 title triumph.

Jack Southworth, 1893/94 – 27 goals
His six goals in the one game against West Bromwich Albion obviously helped to bump up his total.

Alf Milward, 1895/96 – 17 goals
In total, Milward scored 97 goals in 224 games for Everton, a total that any striker would be proud of, never mind a winger.

Jock Proudfoot, 1898/99 – 13 goals
In his first season following a £100 transfer from Blackburn, the ex-Partick striker topped the goalscoring chart for Everton. He would be edged out by the more prolific Jack Taylor and Jimmy Settle in future seasons though.

John Brearley, 1902/03 – 8 goals
Brearley was the Alan Harper of his day in that he was extremely versatile and played in a number of positions for the Blues. 1902/03 obviously wasn't the most entertaining of seasons though, given that he was Everton's top scorer with a rather meagre eight goals.

Bill Kirsopp, 1919/20 – 14 goals
In the first season that league football was resumed after the Great War, the Liverpool-born Kirsopp, who won a champions' medal in 1915, scored 14 times from inside right.

Charlie Crossley, 1920/21 – 18 goals
Crossley only had a couple of seasons with Everton before moving to West Ham.

Stanley Fazackerley, 1921/22 – 12 goals
Fazackerley was a record signing for Everton when they paid Sheffield United £4,000 for his services. He repaid them with 21 goals in 57 appearances in total.

Billy Williams, 1922/23 – 13 goals
Williams's best season in front of goal for Everton saw him level with Wilf Chadwick at the top of the club's list of goalscorers.

Tommy White, 1933/34 – 14 goals
Injury to Dixie Dean gave someone else a look in – in this instance, White, who became a docker in later life and sadly died as a result of injuries he received while working on the Liverpool waterfront.

Nat Cunliffe, 1935/36 – 23 goals
Another good striker whose Everton career was rather overshadowed by the presence of Dixie Dean, although he did enough to earn himself one England cap in 1936.

— SHIRT SPONSORS —

1979–85	HAFNIA (purveyors of tinned meats)
1985–95	NEC (electronics company)
1995–97	DANKA (photocopier manufacturer)
1997–2002	One2One (mobile phone company)
2002–04	KEJIAN (electronics company)
2004–present	Chang (Thai brewery)

— AN UNLIKELY SCOURGE —

Jim Melrose is the only player to have scored hat-tricks against Everton for two different clubs. In the 1980s he managed the feat for both Coventry City and Charlton Athletic.

— KINKY BOOTS —

Alan Ball first wore his famous white boots in Everton's 1970 Charity Shield win over Chelsea at Stamford Bridge. His contract with manufacturers Hummel was worth £2,000, but despite the fact that they are still talked about to this day Ball wasn't quite the most appreciative model. He said of the boots, "To be honest they were crap, like cardboard, so I got the young apprentices to paint my Adidas football boots white. It was great, until one day it rained and the black came through. A not-too-happy watching Hummel rep saw what I'd done so I said goodbye to the two grand."

— ROCKY, ROCKY, ROCKY —

One of the most surreal sights ever witnessed at Goodison came before the Blues played a league match with Reading on 14th January 2007. A new Everton director, Robert Earl, one of the men behind the Planet Hollywood restaurant chain, invited one of his celebrity friends to the match, and so it was that Sylvester Stallone, wearing an Everton coat, walked out to the centre circle and held a scarf aloft as the whole crowd chanted "Rocky, Rocky, Rocky".

Several days later he was photographed at the Paris premiere of *Rocky Balboa* still proudly wearing the scarf.

In a parallel with Rocky's first fight with Apollo Creed, Everton got off the canvas in the match to force a battling 1–1 draw after being behind for much of the game.

— 24 HOURS FROM TULSA —

The North American Soccer League attracted plenty of stars and perhaps not so stellar names from all around the world in the late 1970s and early 1980s. A fair share of ex-Evertonians tried their luck over the pond, with the Tulsa Roughnecks being a particularly popular destination – Terry Darracott, Viv Busby, David Irving, Dave Johnson and Duncan McKenzie all had spells there. Perhaps they thought that with a name like that they would be reminded of the Liverpool nightlife they left behind.

— PREMIER LEAGUE DEBUT GOALSCORERS —

Barry Horne v Sheffield Wednesday, 15th August 1992 – Everton's first Premier League goal was a screamer of an equaliser from new signing Horne.

Gary Speed v Newcastle United, 17th August 1996 – Another Welshman, Speed, was far more prolific than Horne and he started how he meant to go on. He scored 18 goals from midfield in the next couple of seasons before he left Goodison under a cloud. His victims in his first game, Newcastle, were to be the eventual beneficiaries of his falling out with Howard Kendall as he went on to give them six great years of service following his transfer to St James' Park.

Mikael Madar v Crystal Palace, 10th January 1998 – Brought in on a free transfer by Kendall, the French target man was almost the definition of the moody foreign striker. He started promisingly, netting in a 3–1 win at Selhurst Park, and went on to score some vital goals as the Blues managed to stay up by the skin of their teeth. New manager Walter Smith, who arrived in the summer, had no time for the long-haired French international though and he was released within a year of his arrival.

Brian McBride v Tottenham, 12th January 2003 – White Hart Lane was a bogey ground for so long for Everton that they could even score three goals there and still manage to lose, as they did on this occasion, 4–3. One of the Blues' scorers was US international McBride who enjoyed a good three-month loan spell with the club. David Moyes ultimately chose not to make the move permanent though, something he may have regretted given that the player prospered at Fulham and developed a rather irritating knack of scoring against Everton.

James Vaughan v Crystal Palace, 10th April 2005 – Vaughan's record-breaking strike should have heralded the arrival of a superstar. However, the extremely talented youngster has only managed to show his ability in short spells thanks to a number of serious injuries.

Andy Johnson v Watford, 19th August 2006 – Following his £8.6 million transfer from Crystal Palace, the pressure was on Johnson to score goals for the Blues, and plenty of them. After a pre-season where he failed to find the net in a succession of friendlies he managed to notch a deflected effort 15 minutes into his Premier League debut against the Hornets at Goodison Park. That was then the springboard for a very productive season in front of goal.

Ayegbeni Yakubu v Bolton Wanderers, 1st September 2007 – Another record capture, the Nigerian international cost David Moyes £11.25 million from Middlesbrough. A mere ten minutes into his debut at the Reebok Stadium he converted a simple chance and went on to finish his first season at Everton with 21 goals in total.

— WAS IT SOMETHING WE SAID? —

Premier League red cards shown, in games against Everton, to players who had played or would play for the Blues themselves.

Date	Player dismissed
5th March 1994	Graeme Sharp (Oldham Athletic)
15th March 1995	Terry Phelan (Manchester City)
13th January 1996	Mark Hughes (Chelsea)
27th September 1999	Sander Westerveld (Liverpool)
23rd August 2000	Carl Tiler (Charlton Athletic)
19th May 2001	Don Hutchison (Sunderland)

— 38 IS THE MAGIC NUMBER —

38 is the highest squad number worn by an Everton player in a first-team game. It belonged to Victor Anichebe during the 2005/06 season and Anderson da Silva Franca the season after that.

Bjarni Viðarsson was assigned the number 41 during the 2006/07 campaign but never made a first-team appearance.

— BELLEFIELD —

9th October 2007 marked the end of an era when David Moyes led the last ever training session at Everton's famous Bellefield training ground in the West Derby area of Liverpool. The completion of a new custom-built facility, Finch Farm in Halewood, heralded a new dawn as the club had outgrown the increasingly dated Bellefield, the place where some of the club's finest players and managers had put in the hard work behind the scenes needed to produce great team performances on Saturday afternoons.

Before the Second World War, Everton had done all their training at Goodison, but in 1946 they began to split their preparation between there and Bellefield, a sports ground previously used for recreation by the staff of the White Star Line and then the Co-op.

In 1964 it was decided that the club's training would take place solely at Bellefield and £130,000 was spent purchasing the land and installing the most modern facilities of the day.

It was opened by Sir Joseph Richards, president of the Football League, on 12th July 1966 and put Everton at the forefront of the British game when it came to such facilities. Indeed, prospective signings often spoke of how impressed they were when they visited.

A delegation from the Brazilian national team, who played at Goodison in the 1966 World Cup, were said to have been so impressed with Bellefield when they paid a visit that they used the design as the basis for a new training complex back in South America.

— WHAT IS IT GOOD FOR? —

Everton were champions at the outbreak of both World Wars, when league football was suspended and only regional competitions were played. If it wasn't for the Kaiser and the Führer, who knows how many more trophies might have been picked up by teams containing greats like Bobby Parker, Harold Makepeace, Tommy Lawton, TG Jones, Joe Mercer and Ted Sagar?

— A RARE THANKS TO THE REDS —

Everton's second league title win came in the 1914/15 season. Bobby Parker was the Blues' star man, scoring 35 league goals – including a hat-trick in a 5–0 win at Anfield – although his exploits alone weren't enough to bring the championship to Goodison for the first time since 1891.

Oldham Athletic were the Toffees' main rivals – they won 4–3 at Goodison in March 1915 – and when Burnley and Sheffield Wednesday turned Everton over at home in April, the Latics looked favourites for the title. Everton's task was made even more difficult by the fact that they faced four away games on the trot before the final match at home to Chelsea.

However, showing great determination and focus, the Blues won all four matches, at Sunderland, West Bromwich Albion, Bradford Park Avenue and Manchester City.

So, on the final day of the season, Everton and Oldham were all square. Remarkably, after doing all the hard work on the road in the previous four games, Everton then conspired to try and throw the title away as they saw their 2–0 lead, thanks to goals from Parker and Tom Fleetwood, pegged back to 2–2 in the closing stages of the match. At Boundary Park though, Fred Pagnam's double for Liverpool sunk Oldham and made Everton champions by a single point.

	P	W	D	L	F	A	Pts
Everton	38	19	8	11	76	47	46
Oldham	38	17	11	10	70	56	45

— A PROPER INCENTIVE —

"Most of the players lived near to the ground, many of them in Goodison Avenue behind the Stanley Park End. It meant that the likes of Dean, Dunn, Stein and even old trainer Harry Cooke would walk to the game with the fans. If you got beat, you stayed in the dressing room for two hours after the match, frightened to go out and face the walk home"
Gordon Watson

— EVERTON LEGENDS: DAVE HICKSON —

Dave Hickson: always gave everything for the cause

There have been few more distinctive figures to turn out for Everton than Goodison's undisputed hero of the 1950s, Dave Hickson. It was a barren decade for the Blues (indeed, they were relegated in 1951 and spent three seasons in the Second Division) and in such times the supporters look for something to cling to for a bit of hope. In this case it was Hickson, an all-action centre forward, with the most impressive quiff of blond hair, who was always guaranteed to give everything for the Everton cause.

Originally from Ellesmere Port, Hickson had been coached

by the Wirral's and indeed Everton's greatest player, Dixie Dean, when he served his two years of National Service with the Cheshire Cadets. Hickson always said that he benefited greatly from that experience, and that his fearsome ability in the air owed much to the tutelage of the old master. His commitment and bravery were all his own, though, and one game in particular sums him up better than any other.

Valentine's Day 1953 saw Second Division Everton host league champions Manchester United in the fifth round of the FA Cup in front of over 77,000 people. United took the lead before Hickson set up Tommy Eglington for the equaliser, but that was just the beginning of the action. A knock to the face saw a bloody gash open up over Hickson's eye and the injury was made worse when the man they called the Cannonball Kid then bravely headed a corner against an upright. His aggressive nature on the pitch – totally belying the fact that he was always a softly spoken gentleman off it – saw him defy the referee's attempts to get him to leave the field as blood poured down his shirt from the ugly wound. And on 63 minutes, with the crowd whipped into a frenzy by his bravery and belligerence, Hickson smashed the winner past Ray Wood. It's no wonder then that he is so often described as a real Roy of the Rovers.

Hickson was sold to Aston Villa in 1955 but returned to Everton in 1957 before sensationally crossing Stanley Park to play for Liverpool, for whom he scored 37 goals in 60 games, but still Evertonians forgive him! How could they not when his most famous quotation is this: "I would have broken every bone in my body for my other clubs, but I would have died for Everton."

Dave Hickson factfile
Born: Ellesmere Port, 30th October 1929
Appearances: 243
Goals: 111
Other clubs: Aston Villa, Huddersfield Town, Liverpool, Cambridge City, Bury, Tranmere Rovers, Ballymena, Ellesmere Port, Northwich Victoria, Winsford United, Fleetwood Town
Full international appearances while at Everton: 0

— INTER AND THEN OUT —

Everton's first game in the European Cup in 1963 saw them rather unluckily draw the mighty Inter Milan in the first round. 62,000 turned up at Goodison to see the Italians give a masterly footballing display to take a goalless draw back to the San Siro. So impressive were Helenio Herrera's team that they were given a standing ovation at the final whistle.

Everton themselves received plaudits from the Argentine following the return leg, clinched by a solitary goal from the Brazilian Jair. The game is most commonly remembered, though, as the one in which Colin Harvey, one of the club's greatest servants but then a raw 18-year-old, was thrown in at the deep end for a debut that even he never expected. "I just thought I was along to carry the skips," he later said of his trip to Italy.

— GROUNDS FOR COMPLAINT —

One of the most loyal employees Everton have ever had was Dougie Rose, the groundsman who joined the club in 1947 and even lived in a house at Bellefield for 50 years. Over the years though, he liked to cut more than the grass down to size. According to Colin Harvey: "All of the youth coaching sessions used to be taken by Les Shannon. One night, we had a game afterwards and I remember there was a great big centre forward who was knocking people all about and scoring all the goals. He was frightening. I thought to myself that I could never be as good as him because he was really physical. So I asked Les who the big guy was and he explained to me that it was Dougie Rose, the groundsman. The coaches just let him join in the game, but he was 12–15 years older than us. He was a grown man with a beard and everything and he used to give the young defenders a torrid time."

— A GOOD DRINK INTERRUPTED
BY THE MATCH —

There can't be many grounds in England with more public houses in staggering distance from them than Goodison. There's none of that 'No away fans' nonsense either, like you get at many places, and for that reason Goodison has to be one of the favourite destinations for the more sociable away fans. Amongst others, they can choose from the following fine hostelries:

Orry's Wine Bar
Crofts Social Club
The Harlech Castle
The Hermitage
The Winslow
The Top House
The Elm Tree
The Spellow
The Royal Oak
Walton Taxi Club
The Albany
The Westminster
The Royal Oak
The County
The Abbey
The Glebe
The Chepstow
The Springfield
The Pacific
The Black Horse
The Stuart

— HOUSEWARMING —

Goodison Park was officially opened on 24th August 1892. The first game, though, didn't take place until 2nd September, when Everton beat Bolton Wanderers 4–2 in a friendly. The first league encounter took place the following day, when Everton drew 2–2 with Nottingham Forest in front of 14,000 spectators.

— NOT SO GOLDEN BROWN —

Scottish full back Sandy Brown is, unfortunately for him, best remembered for the flying header he put into his own net in a 3–0 derby defeat at Goodison in December 1969. Indeed, whenever anyone has done anything remotely similar since – Phil Neville's own goal at Anfield in 2006 was particularly uncanny – it is immediately labelled 'a Sandy Brown'. Less well known though, sadly for Sandy, was that he had scored at the other end against the old enemy, back in August 1966, with the Blues 2–1 up thanks to a brace from Alan Ball. In doing so, Brown, who was on for Fred Pickering, not only sealed the 3–1 win but also became the first ever Everton substitute to score.

"I remember looking up at the Goodison Park clock. It was three o'clock and there were no nerves. I was loving every moment of this as this was my stage. The image of that famous old clock will never leave me. When I looked back at it again it was twelve minutes past three and I had scored two goals."
Alan Ball

— A WARM WELCOME —

"You're that young Lawton aren't you? You'll never be as good as Dixie."
The conductor of the number 4 tram greeting a 17-year-old Tommy Lawton as he made his way to Goodison for the first time.

The youngster had been a goalscoring machine at Burnley and despite the reservations of the tram conductor he would go on to become one of English football's all time legends. He scored 72 goals in 98 top flight games for the Toffees between 1937 and 1945 plus 152 goals in 114 games played during the Second World War.

The penalty he converted in a 2–1 win at Anfield on 2nd October 1937 makes him the youngest ever derby goalscorer, at 17 years and 362 days.

— EVERTON 9 MANCHESTER CITY 1 —

Perhaps unsurprisingly, this win, on 3rd September 1906, ranks as Everton's biggest in the top flight, although they did repeat the same scoreline against Plymouth Argyle in the Second Division in 1930.

This was the first game at Goodison of the 1906/07 season, and as FA Cup holders with a fine team that included the likes of Jack Sharp, Alex 'Sandy' Young, Harry Makepeace and Walter Abbott, Everton were obviously confident. No one expected the deluge of goals that would ensue though. They were five up at half-time through goals from Jack Taylor, two for Jimmy Settle, and one apiece from Abbott and Young. Young bagged another two after the break, Hugh Bolton grabbed another, City scored a very scant consolation effort, and then Young scored his fourth to make it an astonishing nine goals to Everton.

— A DARK NIGHT AT HIGHBURY —

After qualifying for the following season's Champions League by beating Newcastle at Goodison on Saturday 1st May 2005, Everton travelled to Arsenal on the Wednesday in jubilant mood. It appeared that the players had been celebrating even harder than the fans though, as the Blues fell to their heaviest ever Premiership defeat. Beach balls and songs about European tours started to look a bit inappropriate as goals from Robin van Persie, Robert Pires (two), Patrick Vieira, Edu, Dennis Bergkamp and Matthieu Flamini saw Everton go down 7–0.

— IN WITH A BULLET —

Everton's 1985 FA Cup Final song, *Here We Go,* comes in at number 33 in the all-time football record charts, sandwiched between Jean-Michel Jarre and Apollo 440's *Rendez-Vous 98,* used by ITV for the World Cup, and Simply Red's *We're in This Together*, the official song of Euro 96.

The seminal *Anfield Rap (Red Machine in Full Effect)* ranks at number 16.

— GOODISON'S THE NAME —

If Everton do move to a new stadium, something that's been mooted for about the last 20 years, the name will be sold to the highest bidder, as has become the custom in today's increasingly commercialised world. In 1892 though, it was far simpler. George Mahon's new ground was being built on Mere Green Field which was adjacent to Goodison Road, believed to be named after a civil engineer, George William Goodison, who had given a report on sewage to the local council in 1868. How glamorous.

In the minutes from a board meeting on 27th June 1892 it states merely: 'Resolved that football ground be called Goodison Park'.

— SMALL ADS —

Some of the adverts in the programme from Everton's first league season in 1888/89:

WM Railton, jeweller, selling English watches of all descriptions, as well as the newest designs in cups and medals, suitable for cricket, football and rounders.

D Griffiths and Son, pianos tuned and repaired, as well as popular sheet music for 2d.

John Leary, economical undertaker and funeral carriage proprietor.

Dancing at the Royal Assembly Rooms, Breck Road, with select classes held on Monday, Wednesday and Saturday evenings at 8pm.

Grant and Sons, pianos from £5, Organs from £4 and harmoniums from only £3.

— CLASSIC MATCHES:
EVERTON 4 TOTTENHAM 1, 1995 —

The omens were good for this semi-final at Elland Road on 9th April 1995, thanks to Royal Athlete winning the Grand National the previous day. Evertonians had felt like they were destined for Wembley for a while though, as Joe Royle's *athletes* had been treating every match like a cup tie as they sought top-flight survival in the league.

Gerry Francis's Spurs, containing the likes of Jürgen Klinsmann, Teddy Sheringham, Nick Barmby and Darren Anderton, were meant to be too slick for the more prosaic Blues though, and many pundits predicted a 'dream final' featuring the North Londoners and Manchester United.

They never figured on Royle's Dogs of War, though, and the incredible backing from the Evertonians who had been assigned three sides of the ground, making it feel like a little piece of Goodison over in Yorkshire.

According to Gary Mabbutt, "They didn't allow us to play our game. We've had a lot of acclaim this season but won nothing." Everton simply overwhelmed their opponents with a relentless, high-tempo approach. The only surprise was that it took as long as 35 minutes for Matt Jackson – who only really played because Earl Barrett was cup-tied – to glance home Andy Hinchcliffe's corner. Graham Stuart then doubled the lead on 55 minutes, steering home the rebound when Ian Walker – the son of Mike, the manager who Everton had sacked earlier in the season – saved Paul Rideout's initial effort.

Spurs were then awarded a ludicrous penalty that Klinsmann converted on 63 minutes – the only goal the Blues conceded during the whole cup run. Then came the real drama.

There was the real prospect of Tottenham staging a fightback with the scores at 2–1, and Everton's cause didn't seem to be helped by an injury to Rideout. Legend has it that a mix-up then occurred, as the targetman wanted more time to run his knock off, but Royle misinterpreted the physio's signal from the far side of the pitch and sent on substitute Daniel Amokachi. The Nigerian had something of a cult following at Everton, thanks to his energetic, bustling style, but his finishing had left a lot to be desired since his big money move to Goodison and he'd found opportunities thin on the ground once Royle took over.

After the match, the manager would say of the mix-up, "What a good mistake," as Amokachi coolly converted two breakaway goals in the 82nd and 90th minutes to send the euphoric Evertonians to Wembley.

"Sorry for ruining your 'dream final'."
Joe Royle, addressing the press after the match

— A UNIQUE TREBLE —

The Blues put together quite an unusual run after being relegated in the 1929/30 season. They won the Second Division title the following season (1930/31), the First Division championship the season after that (1931/32), and then finished the next campaign by winning the 1933 FA Cup. The chances of anyone emulating even the first two parts of that nowadays, becoming champions after being promoted, seems unlikely in the extreme.

— THE FIRST DERBY —

If only they could have all been like this. On 13th October 1894, Everton finally faced the team that grew up out of their ashes when they departed Anfield. John Houlding's Liverpool had been promoted from the Second Division and, although their second strings had already faced each other, this was the first fully fledged Merseyside derby.

Anticipation of the encounter was great, as 44,000 turned out to watch Everton outclass a rather robust Liverpool side. According to one contemporary report, 'If Liverpool were a little less unscrupulous in their tactics, they would be a popular team.' Unfortunately they became extremely popular while persisting with their underhand ways for over a century.

Goals from Thomas McInness, Alex Latta and John Bell secured a 3–0 victory for the rather more gentlemanly Everton.

— EVERTON ON THE TELLY —

Rocky O'Rourke
One episode of the gritty 1976 kids' drama saw the hero of the title, played by Michael Mills, attend the Goodison derby.

Multi-Coloured Swap Shop
Duncan McKenzie appeared on the Saturday morning children's show in 1977 with a host of stuff to give away. Pride of place went to Bob Latchford's League Cup Final shirt, though, and almost every Evertonian of a certain age remembers ringing in trying to win it.

Our Day Out
Willy Russell's 1977 *Play for Today* about a school trip to North Wales featured one kid in a Blues scarf who tries to teach the café owner's parrot to say "Everton".

Super Teams
A short-lived spin-off from the better-known *Superstars* saw Everton's 1978 side beat Ipswich Town to the inaugural Brylcreem Trophy.

Tiswas
A group of Evertonians, on their way to the League Cup semi-final against West Ham in 1980, are clearly visible in the background while the famous *Bucket of Water* song is being sung.

Home and Away
Not the day-to-day adventures of Australian teenagers but the 1984 Granada documentary following Everton and Liverpool fans on their way to the League Cup Final.

Songs of Praise
In May 1997 over 5,000 local children sang hymns for the Sunday evening religious show from Goodison Park.

Dockers
Jimmy McGovern and Irvine Welsh's drama about the Liverpool dockers' strike had a scene where the main characters hear about Robbie Fowler and Steve McManaman's goal celebration whereby

they raised their shirts to reveal pro-dockers T-shirts. The 'hilarious' joke is that Everton players are going to join in too but they are still waiting to score.

Airline
Boisterous Evertonians on their way to a pre-season friendly at Anderlecht in 2002 can be heard singing as the steward attempts to pluckily point out the exits, etc.

Who Wants to Be a Millionaire?
Evertonian Andy Martin, *en route* to £250,000, phoned a friend whom he described to Chris Tarrant as "a good Blue". A man can give no higher accolade.

The League of Gentlemen
In the series two finale of a show that was known for being bizarre, a man wearing the dreadful 1995 Everton away kit is part of a crazed mob chasing the mayor of Royston Vasey, played by Roy 'Chubby' Brown.

— A BOY NAMED EVERTON —

Everton Weekes OBE – Distinguished West Indian cricketer. The English spin bowler Jim Laker apparently told him, "It's a good job your father wasn't a West Bromwich Albion fan."

Everton Blender – Award-winning reggae singer and producer.

Everton Augusto de Barros Ribeiro and Everton Cardoso da Silva – Brazilian footballers.

Everton Fox – Ex-BBC weather presenter.

Clive Everton – Welsh snooker commentator.

Mark Everton Walters – The king of the pointless step-over, he actually turned the Blues down in favour of Liverpool.

— THE OTHER ALEX YOUNG —

The Golden Vision of the 1960s was not the first Alex Young to ply his trade up front for Everton. The first, Alex 'Sandy' Young, another Scot, signed from Falkirk in July 1901 and went on to become the club's fourth highest goalscorer of all time, with 125 in 314 games. That's 36 more than his more famous namesake.

Young scored four goals in Everton's biggest ever top-flight victory, the 9–1 against Manchester City, as well as the only goal in the 1906 FA Cup Final. He was the Blues' highest scorer five seasons running, between 1903/04 and 1907/08, and topped the league's scoring chart in 1906/07. Most notable in that campaign was a brace in a 2–1 win at Anfield, although Young's greatest triumph against the Reds was when he scored four against them in a 5–2 win on 1st April 1904.

He left Everton for Tottenham in 1911 but failed to settle there or at any of his subsequent clubs. Young emigrated to Australia in 1914, where his life took a tragic turn. Some mystery surrounds his fate, with some stories saying that he was hanged for cattle theft. However, it is more commonly believed that he was found guilty of the manslaughter of his own brother and served time in prison and then a mental hospital before eventually returning to Scotland where he died in 1959.

— BUNCH OF ANIMALS —

David 'Rhino' Unsworth
John 'Tiger' McLaughlin
Robert 'Bunny' Bell
Ayegbeni 'the Yak' Yakubu
Kevin 'the Rat' Ratcliffe
Harry 'the Cat' Catterick
Mike Lyons

— EVERTON LEGENDS: BRIAN LABONE —

Brian Labone: 'footballer, gentleman, Evertonian'

Brian Labone won two league titles and an FA Cup with Everton. He played more games for the club than any other outfield player and won 26 caps for England. However, mere statistics, while impressive, do not do justice to the man who Harry Catterick declared "the last of the Corinthians".

It might have been very different for this Everton legend, as he was torn between football and university before eventually joining the Blues at the age of 17. Famously he excelled in a trial game in 1957, marking no less than Dave Hickson, and was placed straight into the reserve side.

Labone's nature as a gentleman, only booked twice in his career, disguised his strength of character somewhat. In only his second senior game he was given a torrid time by Tottenham's uncompromising Bobby Smith, but Labone didn't let that knock his confidence and by the 1959/60 season he was a first team regular. Indeed, in the 1962/63 season, as well as his first champions' medal he also received his first cap for England – the first Everton player to get one since the war.

In 1966, he replaced Tony Kay as club captain and lifted the FA Cup at Wembley. He didn't return to the Twin Towers in the summer with England though, choosing instead to concentrate on his wedding plans rather than be Jack Charlton's understudy at the World Cup. Then, in 1967, at the tender age of 28, Labone shocked everyone by announcing that he planned to retire from football and go into the family business in 18 months' time, or sooner if the club could find a replacement. This decision was due to a dip in his form, but while he played out his contract his performances improved markedly and, to the delight of the Everton faithful, he changed his mind and led his beloved Blues to another championship in 1969/70. Another World Cup year had come around too, and this time Labone went to Mexico with England and played well as they made it to the quarter-finals.

In 1971 an Achilles' injury forced his retirement from the game, although he remained a familiar face around the club, working in the commercial department and also on the hospitality side on matchdays. He died unexpectedly in 2006, aged only 66, and the thousands who turned up for his funeral at the Anglican cathedral in Liverpool showed the high regard that everyone in the city held him in.

"Three words sum up Brian: footballer, gentleman and Evertonian."
Bill Kenwright, Everton chairman

Brian Labone factfile
Born: Liverpool, 23rd January 1940
Appearances: 534
Goals: 2
Other clubs: None
Full international appearances while at Everton: 26 for England

— CLASSIC MATCHES: EVERTON 3 BAYERN MUNICH 1, 1985 —

Of the modern era at least, this is the greatest game played at Goodison Park. Howard Kendall's team had struggled in the first round of the Cup Winners' Cup against University College Dublin, but after scraping through at Goodison they then went on to cruise past Slovan Bratislava and Fortuna Sittard. The semi-final saw them up against a genuine giant of the European game in Bayern, and a hard-fought goalless draw in Munich set up the return on 24th April 1985.

With almost 50,000 packed into Goodison, Kendall's plan was to simply bombard and overwhelm the Germans, with Andy Gray in particular kicking lumps out of the opposing defenders and perhaps lucky to stay on the pitch after one wild swing at Hansi Pflugler. Despite Everton's pressure though, the visitors silenced the crowd momentarily when they took the lead through Dieter Hoeness on 37 minutes – the away goal that everyone dreaded.

According to Graeme Sharp though, Kendall was undeterred at half-time and gave his players some simple instructions. He said: "You're kicking into the Gwladys Street. Get after them, keep after them, get the ball in there and get physical, they don't like it. Do that and the fans behind the goal will suck one in." And so it proved. From two long throws from Gary Stevens, first Gray flicked on for Sharp to equalise before Sharp returned the favour and Gray put Everton into the lead, despite the goalkeeper Jean Marie-Pfaff's protestations. And in the final five minutes, with Bayern pushing for an equaliser that would see them through on away goals, Everton broke, Gray squared a ball to Trevor Steven and he in turn swept a shot past the exposed Pfaff to seal a historic night.

"Mr Kendall, this is not football!"
Bayern coach **Uli Hoeness**

"F**k off!"
The Everton bench, in reply

— ALMOST FORGOTTEN —

As well as being aggrieved at how late Everton always seem to be shown on *Match of the Day*, another common complaint from Evertonians is that BBC presenter and the face of Walkers crisps, Gary Lineker, very rarely seems to acknowledge that he ever played for the Blues.

Granted, he was only at Goodison for one season, 1985/86, but it was the one that established him in the nation's consciousness as an extraordinary goalscorer. He joined Howard Kendall's champions from Leicester City for a record £800,000, and had a big task on his hands replacing the crowd favourite Andy Gray. By the end of the season though he had scored 40 goals in all competitions – the fourth best tally ever by an Everton player (the three better ones all belong to you-know-who). He was also the Professional Footballers' Association and Football Writers' Association Footballer of the Year. However, Everton finished runners up to Liverpool in both the league and the FA Cup, after Lineker gave them the lead at Wembley. He then finished that summer's World Cup in Mexico with the Golden Boot and Kendall subsequently sold him to Barcelona for £2.75 million, a controversial decision that was in some ways vindicated when the title was regained the following season.

— A NEW ADVENTURE —

Everton's first ever foray into Europe, in the Inter-Cities Fairs Cup in 1962, took them as far as the rather exotic East End Park, home of Dunfermline Athletic. A Dennis Stevens goal in the first leg at Goodison gave the Blues the lead in the tie, only for the Scots to triumph 2–0 in the return leg and end Everton's campaign before it really got going. It was a feeling that Evertonians would have to get used to, unfortunately.

— THE MEN IN CHARGE —

1888–89	William E Barclay
1889–1901	Dick Molyneux
1901–18	Will Cuff
1918–19	WJ Sawyer
1919–35	Thomas McIntosh
1936–48	Theo Kelly
1948–56	Cliff Britton
1956–58	Ian Buchan
1958–61	Johnny Carey
1961–73	Harry Catterick
1973–77	Billy Bingham
1977–81	Gordon Lee
1981–87	Howard Kendall
1987–90	Colin Harvey
1990–93	Howard Kendall
1994	Mike Walker
1994–97	Joe Royle
1997–98	Howard Kendall
1998–2002	Walter Smith
2002–present	David Moyes

Prior to 1939, when Theo Kelly became Everton's first 'proper' manager, a panel of directors undertook the team selections and transfers. The individuals named in the pre-war periods above are widely regarded as the most prominent decision-makers.

The following also had spells as caretaker manager:

April–May 1973	Tommy Eggleston
January 1977	Steve Burtenshaw
November 1990	Jimmy Gabriel
Dec 1993–Jan 1994	Jimmy Gabriel
March–May 1997	Dave Watson

— DOWN BUT NOT OUT —

While Everton have spent more seasons in the top flight than any other English club, the fact remains that the Second Division is not completely unknown territory for them. The first time they were relegated was the 1929/30 season, with a team that included the likes of Ted Sagar, Cliff Britton, Sam Chedgzoy and the one and only Dixie Dean. They didn't hang around long though, winning promotion at the first attempt and handing out some veritable thrashings along the way. They put nine past Plymouth, six past Oldham and seven past poor old Charlton Athletic at Goodison and then again at the Valley for good measure.

— DOWN AGAIN —

Everton's second relegation came about at the end of the 1950/51 season. They were undone by some terrible sequences of results, including five straight defeats in October and November and then nine matches without a win from February to the season's penultimate match in April. Unlike the first time when they went down though, in 1930, this team didn't bounce straight back. In fact, they finished seventh then 16th in the next two seasons, before being promoted at the end of the 1953/54 season – and even then in second place behind Leicester City.

— CAN YOU REALLY DIG IT? —

Goodison Park has the distinction of being the first ground in England to have dugouts installed. They were constructed in 1931 and the club got the idea after visiting Aberdeen's Pittodrie, where trainer Donald Colman had pioneered – if that's the right term – the sunken dugout. Colman was said to be keen on boxing and dancing and so wished to better observe the footwork of his players. As a meticulous note-taker he also wanted to keep his writing pad protected from the elements.

— YEARLY AWARDS —

Football Writers' Association Footballer of the Year
1985 Neville Southall
1986 Gary Lineker

Professional Footballers' Association Players' Player of the Year
1985 Peter Reid
1986 Gary Lineker

Manager of the Year
1985 Howard Kendall
1987 Howard Kendall
2003 David Moyes
2005 David Moyes

— EDDIE'S ONE-MAN PITCH INVASION —

There was something about the Wembley pitch in 1966 that almost turned it into a magnet for the fans. Kenneth Wolstenholme famously mentioned the supporters encroaching on the hallowed turf as Geoff Hurst sealed the World Cup for England, but an Evertonian, Eddie Cavanagh, beat them to it when Mike Trebilcock scored his second goal and drew Everton level with Sheffield Wednesday in that year's FA Cup Final.

The famous footage shows Cavanagh, a renowned Blue who had spent time on the club's books as a youngster, running on to the pitch to celebrate with Trebilcock before being pursued by a pair of policemen. In true Keystone Cops fashion, the first seizes the intruder by the jacket, only for him to slip out of it and keep running in his shirtsleeves and braces. The second constable rugby-tackles him to the ground, though, before Brian Labone and Gordon West plead with the officers to take it easy on him. Although they threw him out of the ground, Cavanagh insisted in later interviews that he managed to bunk back in to see Derek Temple's winner and the presentation of the cup.

— EVERTON AGAINST THE NAZIS —

Six years before England's footballers famously gave the fascist salute before a game against Germany, Everton's players had shown more courage and defiance. It was 1932 and a pre-season tour of German kicked off with a game in Dresden, watched by Herman Göring and Joachim von Ribbentrop. Dixie Dean is said to have instructed the players not to give the one-armed salute and they followed their captain's lead, despite the jeers and whistles from the home crowd.

— THE FARM —

What it took to put together Everton's Finch Farm training complex:

150 weeks
69,000 ceramic tiles
68,000 ceramic blocks
4,376 carpet tiles
550 tins of paint
265 tonnes of steel
1,400 cubic metres of concrete
14 million pounds sterling

— LEND US YOUR ODDS? —

Visitors to Goodison have always made jokes about the kids in the streets around the ground who ask for money for minding your car. Peter Osgood, though, was once almost reduced to joining them, in order to raise some cash for his train fare home. The ex-Chelsea legend was playing for Norwich, on loan from Southampton, when the Canaries were defeated 3–1 by the Blues on 19th April 1977. After the match, John Bond, the Norwich boss, asked Osgood to see if Southampton would extend the loan. When Osgood refused, Bond wouldn't let him on the team bus and left him stranded outside Goodison on his own.

— A BRIEF HISTORY OF GOODISON PARK —

There is much talk nowadays of Everton leaving Goodison Park, a ground that is felt to be ageing and in some areas barely adequate for modern football. For a long time, though, it was the country's foremost football stadium – in fact, it was the first properly developed stadium in England and only really pre-dated anywhere by the homes of the Old Firm up in Glasgow.

Goodison was officially opened by Lord Kinnaird and Frederick Wall of the FA on 24th August 1892 and, although impressive then, was developed and improved continuously, right up until 1994 when the present Park End stand was opened. An indication of how impressive a venue Goodison was came when the FA Cup Final was staged there in 1894, making it the first league ground to have that honour.

The Gwladys Street Stand

Probably the most famous of Goodison's stands, the Gwladys Street, at the north end of the ground, was the last to become two-tiered when it was rebuilt in 1938, making Goodison the first ground in the country to have double-decked stands on all sides. Opened by King George VI and Queen Elizabeth, it cost £50,000 to construct. Unfortunately, the Luftwaffe seemed to believe that Goodison was a factory and bombed the ground during the Second World War. The new Gwladys Street Stand took the brunt of the explosions and Everton subsequently received £5,000 from the War Damage Commission with which to make repairs.

Some opposing players would probably sympathise with the German bomber pilots as the Gwladys Street unfortunately has something of a reputation when it comes to missiles being thrown onto the pitch. Indeed, footage from the 1960s shows how a large semicircle was removed from the front of the Gwladys Street and Park End stands to try to afford some protection to opposing goalkeepers.

The Main Stand

In 1909 Archibald Leitch's Goodison Road two-tiered stand was built, incorporating the club's offices and changing rooms. It was the largest grandstand in the country at the time and cost £8,000 to build, but it was replaced in 1971 by the immense triple-decker

EVERTON

Home and Away Kits

1878-2009

www.historicalkits.co.uk

1878-80

1880-81

1881-83

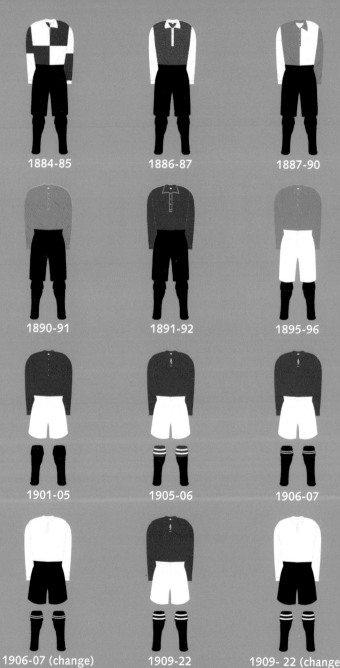

1884-85

1886-87

1887-90

1890-91

1891-92

1895-96

1901-05

1905-06

1906-07

1906-07 (change)

1909-22

1909- 22 (change)

1922-23

1922-23 (change)

1926-29

1926-29 (change)

1929-30

1929-33 (change)

1930-31

1931-32

1932-33

1933 (FA Cup Final)

1934-39

1947

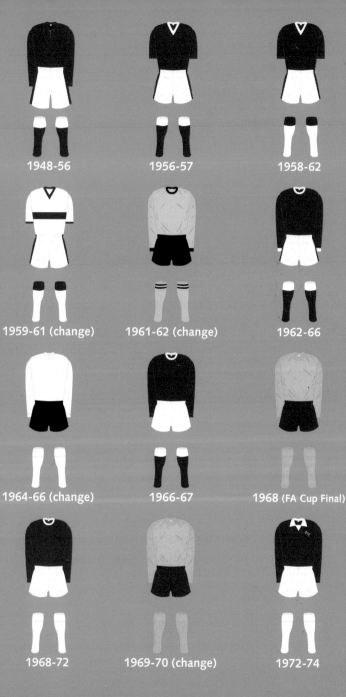

1948-56

1956-57

1958-62

1959-61 (change)

1961-62 (change)

1962-66

1964-66 (change)

1966-67

1968 (FA Cup Final)

1968-72

1969-70 (change)

1972-74

1972-74 (change)

1972 (third)

1974-76

1975 (change)

1976-77

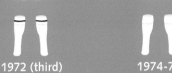
1977-78

1977-78 (change)

1978-79

1978-79 (change)

1979-81

1979-82 (change)

1981-82

1982-83

1982-83 (change)

1982-83 (third)

1983-85

1983-85 (change)

1983-85 (third)

1984 (FA Cup Final)

1985 (FA Cup Final)

1985-86

1985-86 (change)

1986 (FA Cup Final)

1986-89

1986-88 (change)   **1988-90 (change)**   **1988-1990 (third)**

1989 (FA Cup Final)   **1989-91**   **1990-92 (change)**

1991-93   **1992-94 (change)**   **1992-93 (third)**

1993-95   **1993-94 (third)**   **1994-95 (change)**

1995-97

1995-96 (change)

1995 (FA Cup Final)

1996-97 (change)

1997-99

1997-98 (change)

1998-99 (change)

1998-99 (third)

1999-2000

1999-2000 (change)

2000-02

2000-01 (change)

2000-01 (third)

2001-02 (change)

2001-02 (third)

2002-03

2002-03 (change)

2002-03 (third)

2003-04

2003-04 (change)

2004-04 (third)

2004-05

2004-05 (change)

2004-05 (third)

2005-06

2005-06 (change)

2005-06 (third)

2006-07

2006-07 (change)

2006-07 (third)

2007-08

2007-08 (change)

2007-08
(home change)

2007-08 (third)

2008-09

Main Stand that presently incorporates the Family Enclosure at pitch level, a row of executive boxes, the Main Stand itself, and then the Top Balcony way up in the gods.

Such is its height, the floodlight pylons had to be removed and the lamps themselves were attached to gantries at the front of the stand's roof. The inclusion of escalators up to the Top Balcony give an indication of just how unsuitable it is up there for anyone with vertigo.

Occupying the corner between the Main Stand and the Gwladys Street is a church, of St Luke the Evangelist – a feature that makes Goodison distinct from pretty much every other football stadium in the world.

The Bullens Road Stand
The stand that shows its age more than all the rest is the Bullens Road one, and its facilities, and poor views, which haven't really been improved since it was built in 1926, are the most commonly cited examples when people argue that Everton have outgrown Goodison.

Divided into the upper and lower Bullens, the portion nearest the Park End is where away fans are now seated.

The Park End
Originally a two-tier stand – the first in the country when constructed in 1907 – a new, single-tier cantilevered stand was opened in 1994, seating 6,000 fans. Everton missed a golden opportunity when it was built to make it two-tiered and to include the sort of corporate facilities that the ground lacks in comparison with other, more modern Premier League grounds. The fact that a great deal of the matchday hospitality now takes place in a tent in the car park to the rear of the stand says it all.

The last portion of the ground where standing was allowed was the front section of terracing on the old Park End stand. In the wake of the Taylor Report all stadia had to become all-seater, but because of the intention to redevelop the Park End, the terracing at the front remained for games where the visitors brought a big following – as this was the away end at the time.

A 3–2 extra-time defeat by Bolton Wanderers, in the FA Cup third round replay on 19th January 2004, was the last occasion when supporters stood at Goodison Park.

— WE'LL NEVER KNOW —

Like any football club, Everton has an immense capacity for generating rumours, with someone always knowing a friend of a player, or a taxi driver who had a club director in the back of his cab who just couldn't wait to divulge all sorts of sensitive information. As a result, official announcements from the club are often treated with scepticism, as there is always someone who claims to know the *real* story. Theories abound over the following, for instance:

Why was Alan Ball really sold?

Did Pat Van Den Hauwe really have a blood disorder?

Did Everton really mean to buy Ray Atteveld?

Was a rocking horse really responsible for giving Maurice Johnston a black eye?

Did Andrei Kanchelskis really have to give half of his wages to the Russian mafia?

What was the truth behind Gary Speed's falling out with the club and his subsequent departure?

Why didn't chief executive Trevor Birch stay around long enough to get his business cards printed?

— THE FRONT PAGE —

Some imaginatively titled Everton autobiographies:

Even Stevens	Gary Stevens and Trevor Steven
Shades of Gray	Andy Gray
Royle Flush	Joe Royle
Ball of Fire	Alan Ball
Sharpy: My Story	Graeme Sharp
The Real McCall	Stuart McCall
Strikingly Different	Gary Lineker
Claret and Blues	Tony Cottee
Never Say Dai	Dai Davies

— THE BAN —

First and foremost, it must always be remembered that 39 football fans went to the European Cup Final between Liverpool and Juventus at the Heysel Stadium in 1985 and never came home. That is a tragedy and should never be forgotten.

In the aftermath, English clubs were banned from European competition for an indefinite period – ultimately they were excluded for five years. For Everton, who a fortnight earlier had won their first European trophy in Rotterdam with no hint of trouble, the ban was particularly tough. Their best ever team won the league twice but never got the opportunity to go on and play in the European Cup and earn themselves one of those little gold stars to adorn the front of their shirts. By the time the ban was lifted, the club was on the slide, Howard Kendall had left for Bilbao and some of the best players had departed.

Arguments rage over the significance of the ban, as other clubs managed to cope and go onto bigger and better things. There's an element of truth to that as well, as Everton suffered a great deal of mismanagement in the late 1980s and early 1990s, so not every misfortune can be traced back to Heysel. Blues will always wonder what might have been though, had that wonderful side of the mid-1980s been given the chance they'd earned to play on the biggest stage.

— NO FOWL! —

Neil Robinson was an apprentice at Everton before he turned professional in 1974, made 17 starts and then moved to Swansea in 1979. Rather unusually for a sportsman, and especially in the 1970s, Robinson was a vegan and would only wear football boots that were man-made as opposed to leather.

— THE WORLD CUP AT GOODISON —

Goodison Park has hosted more World Cup games than any other league ground in England, and indeed is the only one to have ever staged a World Cup semi-final. As one of the country's premier venues Goodison featured prominently during the World Cup, hosting group games, a quarter-final and a semi.

Group Three in the qualifying stages featured Portugal, Brazil, Hungary and Bulgaria. The matches were staged in the North-West, divided between Goodison and Old Trafford.

Brazil 2 Bulgaria 0, 12th July 1966

52,000 turned up for the first match on Merseyside and saw free kicks from Brazil's Pelé and Garrincha overcome a cynical Bulgarian side. Pelé's strike – before he was kicked out of the game and forced to miss the next one, against Hungary – gave him the distinction of being the first man to score in three successive World Cups.

Hungary 3 Brazil 1, 15th July 1966

Another massive crowd descended on Goodison for the clash between Brazil and Hungary and got a shock as the Magyars, inspired by Florian Albert, triumphed 3–1.

Portugal 3 Brazil 1, 19th July 1966

The South Americans needed a good result then in their final group game against Portugal to stay in the tournament. Pelé was again the victim of some awful tackling and another striker took centre stage, Portugal's Eusebio, scoring twice in a 3–1 win that sent Brazil home.

Portugal 5 North Korea 3, 23rd July 1966

Portugal returned to Goodison in the quarter-final to face the South Korean team who had pulled off the upset of the tournament by beating Italy 1–0 up at Ayresome Park. They looked like surpassing that feat as well, when they raced to a 3–0 lead in the first 25 minutes against a stunned Portugal. However, that only set the scene for Eusebio, who scored four goals in 32 minutes before José Augusto rounded off one of the great comebacks in World Cup history.

West Germany 2 USSR 1, 25th July 1966
The final match of the tournament to take part at the home of
the Blues saw West Germany beat the Soviet Union 2–1 to set
up that dramatic and memorable final. The legendary Lev Yashin
was between the sticks for the USSR but he was beaten by Helmut
Haller and Germany's own legend, Franz Beckenbauer, before
Valery Porkuyan scored a late consolation for the men from
behind the Iron Curtain.

— GOING LOCO IN THE INTERTOTO —

The 1995/96 season was a relatively good one for Everton. Joe
Royle's FA Cup holders strengthened their side considerably, not
least with the capture of Andrei Kanchelskis from Manchester
United, and the Russian winger's 16 goals were instrumental in
pushing the Toffees up to a highly creditable sixth-place finish.
Normally that would have ensured a place in the following
season's UEFA Cup. However, thanks to Tottenham, Wimbledon
and Sheffield Wednesday fielding weakened sides in the 1995/96
InterToto Cup, European football's governing body saw fit to
deny one UEFA Cup spot to the English clubs for the following
season as punishment. And so Everton missed out.

— SCHOOL OF SCIENCE V THE SWEET SCIENCE —

Sylvester 'Rocky' Stallone wasn't the first boxer ever to take to
the pitch at Goodison. In 1915 a charity match was organised
between an Everton XI – ostensibly the 1906 FA Cup-winning
team – and a boxers' XI. The biggest name for the boxing team
was the British heavyweight champion, Bombardier Billy Wells.
He also had the distinction of being the second ever Gongman
for the Rank Organisation, striking said instrument on screen
at the beginning of their films.

Everton won the game 3–1 in a thankfully even-tempered
encounter.

— THE BLUES —

Everton are commonly known as the Blues, and their royal blue and white strip is probably one of the most famous in English football. However, in the early stages of their history they played in an assortment of garish outfits until in 1901 they settled on something that resembles the colours that have become synonymous with the club.

From 1878 to the end of the 19th century they experimented with piratical-looking blue and white stripes, a black kit with a salmon pink sash that earned the nickname the Blackwatch, salmon and white halves, blue and white halves and quarters, and also plain salmon shirts from 1890 to 1895. It must be noted that the salmon should never, ever be confused for red.

From 1895 to 1901, Everton adopted a light blue shirt with white shorts; that shirt became royal blue in 1901 and the modern kit was more or less born from that point. The socks have alternated between white and blue down the years but the consensus from supporters is almost universally in favour of the white as they bring back memories of the kit worn by the likes of Alan Ball between 1968 and 1972.

EFC was embroidered on the chest of the shirts for a spell in the mid-twenties and then again from 1972, only to be replaced by the club crest in 1978. The late 1970s shirts also featured the iconic Umbro diamonds down the arms, a feature that many fans would like to see reintroduced given that after dalliances with the likes of Le Coq Sportif and Puma, Umbro are once again the manufacturers of the Everton kit.

The Blues have had their share of slightly odd kits too, not least the one worn in 1985/86 campaign that became known as the Lineker bib for the incongruous white panel on the front of the shirt worn during the ex-Leicester marksman's one season at Goodison. The 1990s were the decade that taste forgot in terms of kits and Everton had some horrors, like the 1991–93 shirt with its MC Escher-style geometric patterns, or the truly horrible lighter blue that was used in the 1997–99 shirt. The 1995–97 kit, the one that Everton wore when they won the FA Cup, inexplicably had black panels all over it and awful black and blue stripy socks.

Everton away colours are traditionally considered to be amber shirts and socks with blue shorts, but like all clubs they have, down the years, given sportswear companies free rein to concoct all manner of wacky monstrosities. The 1995/96 effort was probably the worst, a white shirt with a black pattern across the front that gave the distinct impression that a tractor had driven over it.

— THE ALL-TIME PREMIERSHIP TABLE —

As of the end of the 2007/08 season:

	P	W	D	L	Pts
1 Manchester United	620	394	137	89	1319
2 Arsenal	620	332	168	120	1164
3 Chelsea	620	310	168	142	1098
4 Liverpool	620	306	157	157	1075
5 Aston Villa	620	230	187	203	877
6 Newcastle United	578	240	152	186	872
7 Tottenham Hotspur	620	223	165	232	834
8 Blackburn Rovers	544	220	145	179	805
9 Everton	**620**	**211**	**167**	**242**	**800**

— FOUNDER MEMBERS —

Along with Accrington, Aston Villa, Blackburn Rovers, Bolton Wanderers, Burnley, Derby County, Notts County, Preston North End, Stoke, West Bromwich Albion and Wolves, Everton were founder members of the Football League, formed in 1888. Before then, clubs simply played friendlies that they organised on an *ad hoc* basis.

Everton's first league encounter was a 2–1 home win against Accrington, although that wasn't a particularly good indication of how that initial season would pan out. Everton eventually finished eighth, 20 points behind runaway winners Preston.

— CELEBRATE GOOD TIMES, COME ON —

Evertonians are generally a down-to-earth bunch who are suspicious of new trends and any sort of zany behaviour. Rival fans always comment on the lack of clever or supposedly witty songs sung at Goodison and it is almost inconceivable that the Blues would ever spawn any weirdo self-publicist fans like that bloke in the wig at Portsmouth or him with all the badges over at Liverpool. The players seem to realise that too, and on the whole Goodison has seen very little of the choreographed goal celebrations that for a long time have been a scourge of the game. That said, David Unsworth and Stuart Barlow did indulge in a bit of an embarrassing little jig at the City Ground in 1995 and Kevin Campbell was guilty for a while of pretending to scratch a record whenever he scored.

Wayne Rooney celebrated a goal in the FA Youth Cup Final by lifting his shirt to reveal a T-shirt bearing the legend 'Once a Blue always a Blue', a phrase that came back to haunt both him and Evertonians given his acrimonious defection to Manchester United.

When it comes to spontaneous, iconic outpourings of joy though, two in particular spring to mind. First, few people will forget Duncan Ferguson scoring the winner against Manchester United in February 1995 before setting off along the length of the Family Enclosure, twirling his shirt around his head. Even more famous though were Bob Latchford's celebrations when equalising against West Ham towards the end of extra time in the 1980 FA Cup semi-final replay at Elland Road. The Latch leapt onto the railings at the Gelderd End, going just as potty as the hordes of Evertonians before him. Sadly though, in the dying minutes, Frank Lampard Sr struck the winner for the Hammers and performed another famous celebration, running around the corner flag in delight.

"I used to stick the ball in the net and bow three times to the Kop. They never liked me doing that."
Dixie Dean

— EVERYTHING STARTS WITH A ZEE —

Z-Cars. Not half as exciting without the music.

The distinctive music that Everton run out to at Goodison Park, with that drum roll that makes the hairs stand up on the back of your neck before the flute kicks in, is the theme tune to the 1960s television show *Z-Cars,* a gritty police drama based in the fictional North-West town of Newtown. The tune itself, composed by Fritz Speigl, is based on the folk song *Johnny Todd* from the late 19th century. The version played at Everton to this day was released as a single, performed by Johnny Keating and his orchestra, and reached number 5 in the charts in April 1962. The popular belief is that one of the actors from the series, Terence Edmond, was an Evertonian and took a number of the cast to watch a match – thought to have been the 4–1 defeat of Birmingham City in April 1962. In recognition of their presence, the theme music was played over the tannoy before the game and consequently has been ever since, apart from a short spell in 1994 when chairman Peter Johnson had the strange idea of replacing it with *Fanfare for the Common Man.*

Everton aren't the only team to play *Z-Cars* as they take to the pitch though – Sunderland did for a while and Watford still do.

— THE MERSEY MILLIONAIRE —

Although born in Manchester in 1896, Sir John Moores and the Moores family would become synonymous with the city of Liverpool and both of its football clubs for almost a century.

Sir John became enamoured with Everton when he began working as a telegraph boy on Merseyside in the 1920s and was reportedly in the crowd to see Dixie Dean score his record-breaking 60th goal. An enterprising sort, Moores was involved with several entrepreneurial ventures including the importation of golf balls and stationery to County Kerry in Ireland, but the one that would eventually make him his fortune was the idea of a 'football pool' that had been trialled unsuccessfully in Birmingham. Indeed, Moores and his three colleagues who set up Littlewoods Football Pools struggled to make it pay at first too. Encouraged to carry on by his wife, who told him, "I would rather be married to a man who is haunted by failure rather than one haunted by regret," he bought out his co-investors and began to make the scheme pay. By 1932 he was a millionaire and began to diversify, opening his first mail order store that year and then, by 1937, his first department store.

During the Second World War, Moores bought half of the shares in Everton owned by his friend Dick Searle and in the 1950s began helping the club out by lending it money, interest free, to improve the ground and to buy better players. In 1960 he was elected chairman, famously sacked Johnny Carey in a taxi, and then presided over a new dawn for the club as the next decade saw his 'Mersey Millionaires' compete again at the top of the English game.

Although he left the board of directors in 1977, his presence was always a strong one and he attended Everton games, wearing a hand-knitted blue and white scarf given to him by a fan, until he was 90 years old. Indeed, at the age of 89, when he saw Howard Kendall's team crowned champions he declared, "I never thought I'd live to see another championship come to Everton. It's great to feel free of the domination of Liverpool."

— REBUKE AT THE REEBOK —

1st September 1997 and Everton were the very first visitors to Bolton Wanderers' brand new Reebok Stadium. On 57 minutes the home crowd thought they had christened the ground with its first goal when Nathan Blake looked to have forced the ball home from close range, only for referee Stephen Lodge to rule that it hadn't crossed the line. Television replays showed that it had but, in Everton's defence, Lodge also appeared to have missed a foul by Blake on Neville Southall. The net result was that the game finished 0–0 and at the end of the season the bottom of the table finished thus:

	P	W	D	L	F	A	GD	Pts
17 **Everton**	38	9	13	16	41	56	-15	40
18 Bolton Wanderers	38	9	13	16	41	61	-20	40
19 Barnsley	38	10	5	23	37	82	-45	35
20 Crystal Palace	38	8	9	21	37	71	-34	32

— UNUSUAL DECORATIONS —

Fred Kennedy won no honours with Everton during his two-year stint at Goodison in the mid-1920s. He did however win the French league and cup while playing for Racing Club de Paris in 1933. Even more unusual, though, was the Royal Humane Society Medal he was awarded for resuscitating a young woman who he saved from drowning.

— RECORD APPEARANCE MAKERS
(ALL COMPETITIONS) —

1 Neville Southall	751
2 Brian Labone	534
3 Dave Watson	528
4 Ted Sagar	497
5 Kevin Ratcliffe	493

— ONE OF NINE —

Everton's first league title came in the 1890/91 season, the third since the Football League was founded. They had finished the previous campaign only two points behind champions Preston, but a blistering start set them on course to be the first club to break the Lancashire club's dominance. Before losing to Bolton in October, Everton racked up five straight wins and a draw, inspired by the goalscoring of Fred Geary who netted 11 times during that run and would finish the season with 20 goals in total. The top of the table at the end of the season looked like this:

	P	W	D	L	F	A	Pts
1 Everton	22	14	1	7	63	29	29
2 Preston	22	12	3	7	44	23	27

— GET OFF THE PITCH! —

Probably more famous than Andy King's volleyed winner in the Goodison derby on 28th October 1978 is the post-match interview. Amidst delirious scenes, BBC reporter Richard Duckenfield attempted to get King's reaction only for the pair of them to be unceremoniously bundled off the pitch by a rather irate policeman.

— LIVE TRANSMISSION —

Over 100,000 fans paid to watch the FA Cup fifth round game between Everton and Liverpool in March 1967. Almost 70,000 packed into Goodison, while another 40,000 watched the match on giant screens erected over the park at Anfield.

Rumour has it that many of the Reds looked under their seats for the remote control and asked for the channel to be changed when Alan Ball scored what would be the only goal of the game.

— EVERTON LEGENDS:
HOWARD KENDALL (MANAGER) —

Howard Kendall: an Everton icon

Already an Everton icon as a player, Kendall returned to the club to take over from Gordon Lee in 1981 after working wonders at Blackburn Rovers. As player-manager, Kendall took the Lancashire club from Division Three to the cusp of the First Division, only missing out on goal difference at the end of the 1980/81 campaign.

He retained his player registration when he came back to Goodison and an indicator of the state of the playing resources he inherited was that even at the age of 35 he still had to turn out four times. It was far from plain sailing in the early stages, as his initial signings, the now legendary Magnificent Seven, failed to reignite the club's fortunes. Indeed, Everton struggled so badly in the first couple of seasons of Kendall's reign that there were calls for his head and in an infamous and somewhat shameful incident, the words 'Kendall Out' were painted on the doors of his garage.

There are differing opinions on exactly when everything turned around, but the most commonly held one, and indeed Kendall's own, pinpoints the Milk (League) Cup quarter-final at the Manor Ground on 18th January 1984. With under ten minutes remaining, and 1–0 down to a Bobby McDonald goal, Everton were going out of the cup and the feeling was that it was the end of the road for Kendall. That was until Kevin Brock made a slack back pass that changed the course of Everton history. The ever alert Adrian Heath seized on Brock's error, rounded Steve Hardwick in the Oxford goal and fired home the equaliser.

Later, Heath would say, "It's the goal that people talk about the most because it meant so much to people at the time and there was all the talk of it possibly being Howard's last game. If that were true, then I couldn't have repaid his faith in me any better."

From that point on the inconsistent side that Kendall had been building sparked to life and went on to both domestic cup finals that season – eventually losing the Milk Cup to Liverpool after a replay and then beating Watford 2–0 to lift the FA Cup, the first silverware the club had seen for 14 years.

The following season saw Kendall's men sweep to the league title, win the club's first and only European trophy by triumphing in the European Cup Winners' Cup, and just miss out on a treble when they lost the FA Cup Final to Manchester United. Unfortunately, though, Everton were denied the chance to compete in the European Cup thanks to the ban on English clubs in the wake of the Heysel tragedy.

In 1985/86, the Toffees finished runners-up to their neighbours in both the league and the FA Cup, before winning the title again in 1986/87. That was to be the end of Kendall's first spell in charge, though. He was courted by Barcelona for some time, only for them to offer Terry Venables a further year in charge. They had whetted his appetite for European football, though, something he couldn't get in England. Therefore Kendall accepted the offer to take charge of Athletic Bilbao and a glorious era was over at Goodison.

Kendall would return to Everton as manager on two occasions, in 1990 and 1997, declaring his relationship with the club as like a marriage. However, football had changed and the club had gone backwards since those heady days of the mid-1980s and he never came close to recreating the old magic. Nevertheless, he will always be remembered by Evertonians as a great player, their greatest manager, a *bon viveur extraordinaire* and all round living legend.

— BUT NO CIGAR —

Everton have a proud history in the FA Cup, winning the trophy five times, but the Blues have also had more than their fair share of disappointments at finals, finishing as runners-up on no fewer than seven occasions.

Year	Venue	Result
1893	Fallowfield Stadium	Wolves 1 Everton 0
1897	Crystal Palace	Aston Villa 3 Everton 2
1907	Crystal Palace	Sheffield Wednesday 2 Everton 1
1968	Wembley	West Bromwich Albion 1 Everton 0
1985	Wembley	Manchester United 1 Everton 0
1986	Wembley	Liverpool 3 Everton 1
1989	Wembley	Liverpool 3 Everton 2

— 7 9 7 9 8 9 9 7 —

Those figures don't represent some arcane code – like something from *Lost* – they are the shirt numbers, as shown on the Goodison scoreboard, when the Blues trounced Southampton 8–0 in November 1971. Joe Royle (9) scored four, David Johnson (7) grabbed a hat-trick, and Alan Ball (8) netted just the once.

— THE YEARS OF THE CAT —

While other managers from the 1960s, such as Bill Shankly, Matt Busby and Don Revie, are still talked about in glowing terms by the footballing world in general, Everton's Harry Catterick very rarely gets mentioned by anyone other than the supporters of the clubs he managed. This seems unusual given that, in terms of domestic success, his record during that decade was the match, if not better, than that of any of his contemporaries.

After enjoying an unspectacular career as a centre forward for Everton, the Yorkshireman became player-manager at Crewe before making his name at Sheffield Wednesday, who he led to promotion from Division Two in 1959. Not satisfied with that, his Owls then pushed Tottenham hard for the league in 1961.

Results spoke for themselves then, but it was also Catterick's reputation as a disciplinarian that attracted John Moores in April 1961 when he was looking for someone to push Everton beyond what he thought Johnny Carey was capable of achieving. Moores's ruthless approach paid dividends when, at the end of the 1962/63 season, the league title returned to Goodison for the first time since the war. The FA Cup followed in 1966 and then Catterick underlined his greatness by securing a second championship, this time in 1969/70, with a team almost completely rebuilt since his first triumph.

He suffered a heart attack in January 1972, thought to be brought on by the stress of the job as his majestic title-winning side failed to dominate English football in the manner that many predicted. A move upstairs followed before he eventually took over as manager at Preston in 1975. Like another Everton great, Dixie Dean, Catterick passed away at Goodison, on 9th March 1985, following an FA Cup quarter-final against Ipswich Town.

Evertonians certainly value Catterick's legacy but it's often thought that his taciturn nature, in his dealings with the players and press alike – especially in comparison with arch self-publicist Shankly across the way – means that an extremely talented manager's contribution to the game often doesn't get the wider credit that it merits.

— THE EVERTON COLLECTION —

In 2002 Dr David France made a decision to part with a collection of Everton-related memorabilia that had taken him 25 years to assemble. With over 10,000 items included in it, this collection, known as the David France Collection and now the Everton Collection is widely regarded as the most complete of its kind relating to any football club in the world.

Despite a great deal of interest from collectors with a desire to purchase separate parts of the collection at premium prices, Dr France chose to sell his collection to the Everton Charitable Trust at a discounted price so that it would be available for the public to view in its entirety.

Eventually, the collection, which has also been augmented by the club's own collection of memorabilia, will be housed in the record office at Liverpool Central Library while elements of it will be displayed in the city's museums as well as at various exhibitions throughout the city.

Some of the elements of the collections are as follows:

The complete club ledgers

These date, unbroken, from 1886 to 1964 and reveal every aspect of the club's running. They cover such events as the fateful departure from Anfield as well as the eventual settling of the club's colours and the various physical changes that have taken place at Goodison Park down the years.

Over 6,000 programmes

These are from Everton games at home and abroad, in the league, cups, reserve games and various exhibition matches. They date back as far as 1886 and it is estimated that they represent 90% of the games the Blues have ever played.

The earliest programme is from a home game against Astley Bridge played at Anfield on 4th September 1886.

Season tickets

These start from 1881 and there is also a collection of ticket stubs, the oldest of which dates back to a game played against Notts County on 1st May 1890.

Medals
Forty players' medals cover all but the most recent title and FA Cup wins, dating back as far as the club's first league win in 1891.

Photographs
The collection includes many team photos including one from 1881 that is thought to be the oldest in existence.

Cigarette cards
One copy of each of the 312 designs thought to have been produced featuring Everton players between 1897 and 1939.

Autographs
Hundreds of player signatures from down the decades, including the infamous book that the players had to sign when turning up for training in the 1930s.

Letters
Over 200 letters, from 80 different clubs, including an invitation to play a match at Aston Villa in 1888.

"This collection has no match anywhere in the football world. It's a unique record of Everton's history – possibly a history unparalleled by any other club. The collection offers a unique record of the evolution of British football and of the city of Liverpool."
Graham Budd, Sotheby's

— A TALL STORY —

As well as being one of the country's premier football clubs, Everton also have a basketball team playing in the top flight of the British Basketball League. Formed in June 2007, the Everton Tigers (formerly the Toxteth Tigers) play in royal blue and are presently based at the Sports Academy in Sefton Park. As interest in the sport grows, the hope is that they will eventually play their home games at the Liverpool Echo Arena, a venue they have already filled for a match against local rivals the Chester Jets.

— I PREDICT A RIOT —

1895 was an eventful year for Everton for many of the wrong reasons. Not only was there the turnstile fraud, but also a riot that took place at Goodison Park on 28th December. The trouble started when the game against Small Heath was called off after half an hour due to a deluge of rain that was making play farcical, despite the best efforts of both sides.

A number of disgruntled supporters wanted their money back and made their way to the club offices to demand just that. Director George Mahon addressed them and offered everyone a ticket for the replayed match, but that didn't placate the crowd who started throwing stones and smashing the office windows. They then made their way across the stands, causing more damage, until police with drawn batons dispersed the mob before they could carry out their threats to burn the ground down.

— THE OTHER EVERTON —

"You are my Everton, my only Everton . . ."

Except that the mighty Toffees of Merseyside are not the only football club named Everton. The other Everton are Corporación Deportiva Everton de Viña del Mar, founded in Chile in 1909 by visiting British sailors. Known as the Ruleteros ('Roulleters', a reference to the fact that Viña del Mar is a gambling resort), the other Everton play in blue and yellow and although there has never been any formal connection between the Chileans and the club from whom they took their name, there is a small Ruleteros Society, formed by fans in England to try to engender links between the two clubs joined by name but separated by the Atlantic Ocean.

— THE MOONLIGHT DRIBBLERS —

During the early part of their history, Everton had the rather enigmatic nickname of the Moonlight Dribblers. This was because their training sessions in Stanley Park were held at night.

— CURE IN ORANGE —

On 2nd November 1991, Everton travelled down to Kenilworth Road to play Luton in the league. On arrival they realised that the home side's kit, while described as white with blue trim in the league handbook, contained so much blue that it clashed with Everton's normal strip. The Toffees had failed to bring their yellow away kit with them and so the only solution was for them to wear Luton's horrendous orange away shirts.

The kit proved lucky though, as Howard Kendall's side won the game 1–0.

— BEHIND ENEMY LINES —

John Brearley and John Cameron both played for Everton at the beginning of the 20th century and both, incidentally, were transferred to Tottenham Hotspur. Indeed, it was Cameron, who had replaced Frank Brettel as manager at Spurs, who went back to his old club to sign Brearley.

That wasn't the end of their association though, as both men were plying their trade in Germany when the First World War broke out – Brearley with Viktoria 89 Berlin and Cameron with Dresdener SC. As a result they were both interned in the Ruhleben civilian POW camp near Berlin, along with England internationals Fred Spiksley, Samuel Wolstenholme and Steve Bloomer, the Derby County legend whose complimentary words gave birth to Everton's tag as the School of Science.

Cameron was secretary of the Ruhleben Football Association, and organised regular tournaments to entertain the prisoners. With something of a captive audience, crowds of over a thousand watched some of the bigger games played at the camp.

— THAT'S A LOT OF HORSES —

Records show that in preparation for the 1888/89 season, the Anfield pitch was levelled and re-sown. Fifteen tons of horse manure were dumped there in the process.

That could explain a lot.

— GREAT ESCAPES:
EVERTON 3 WIMBLEDON 2, 1994 —

Of all the cup finals, European ties and top of the table league encounters that Everton have ever been involved in, there are few that can claim to have been as dramatic as the final-day league clash with Wimbledon on 9th May 1994.

Norwich's Mike Walker had taken over a struggling Everton in January but then only presided over a further four league wins before the final game. Two teams from five were in the relegation mix, although Everton were the only ones with home advantage, but even that was compromised somewhat by the fact that the Park End was nothing more than a building site.

Controversy always surrounds this game. Hans Segers, the Wimbledon goalkeeper, was questioned about it as part of an investigation into match fixing, while there was also talk of the Dons players being scared of winning, especially after an attempt was made to set their coach on fire the night before the game. Indeed, it's been said that they took to the field with their kit reeking of smoke.

If the visitors were trying to throw the game they did their best to disguise the fact, going 2–0 up within the first 20 minutes. Dean Holdsworth scored a penalty following Anders Limpar's inexplicable handball before Gary Ablett sliced a grotesque effort into his own net.

Limpar atoned for his earlier misdemeanour by diving outrageously to win the penalty that Graham Stuart nervelessly converted to give the Blues a glimmer of hope at half-time.

In the second half, Stuart got away with handling a Holdsworth effort off his own line only moments before the Everton equaliser. Barry Horne, with only one goal to his name in a blue shirt, pushed forward an awkward, bouncing ball in midfield before unleashing a phenomenal swerving shot from 30 yards and watching it nestle in the top corner of the Gwladys Street goal.

However, at that point Everton were still destined for the drop. With the crowd almost beside themselves, urging the players forward for a winner, the moment came that landed Segers in hot water with the authorities. Tony Cottee laid a ball into the path of Stuart, just at the edge of the box, and the midfielder's lunging stab at the ball sent it bobbling apologetically goalwards. Somehow, though, the Dutch keeper – who later stated that a divot in the pitch was to blame – let the ball slip through his hands and into the bottom corner.

Everton clung on for the final ten minutes while late goals conceded at Stamford Bridge saw Sheffield United drop into the final relegation spot. This is how the final table looked:

	P	W	D	L	F	A	GD	Pts
17 Everton	42	12	8	22	42	63	-21	44
18 Southampton	42	12	7	23	49	66	-17	43
19 Ipswich Town	42	9	16	17	35	58	-23	43
20 Sheffield United	42	8	18	16	42	60	-18	42
21 Oldham Athletic	42	9	13	20	42	68	-26	40
22 Swindon Town	42	5	15	22	47	100	-53	30

— SOME FAMOUS FACES WHO APPEARED IN Z-CARS —

Actor	Years	Character
Brian Blessed	1962–65	PC 'Fancy' Smith
Leonard Rossiter	1963	Det Insp Bamber
John Thaw	1963–64	DC Elliot
Colin Welland	1963–65	PC David Graham
Joss Ackland	1964–68	Det Insp Todd

— TOO MUCH CHRISTMAS PUD? —

On Christmas Day 1934, Everton veritably walloped Sunderland 6–2, with the Blues' goals coming from Jackie Coulter, Dixie Dean, Albert Geldard, Alex Stevenson and Jimmy Cunliffe with a brace.

The return fixture was played the following day. Whether the Everton players had overindulged back at home is not known, but the result – a 7–0 win for Sunderland – certainly suggests some of the Blues may not have been in tip-top condition.

— THE REF HAS EYES —

After the remarkable feat of finishing the 2004/05 season in fourth place and securing a spot in the Champions League, Everton had the misfortune of drawing the strongest side in the qualifying round, Spain's Villarreal. A 2–1 defeat at Goodison left David Moyes' men with an uphill struggle when they travelled to El Madrigal Stadium on 24th August 2005. The task was made even more difficult when the slick Spaniards went a goal up in the first half, leaving the Blues chasing two goals just to force extra time.

With 20 minutes left in the match, Mikel Arteta curled home a delightful free kick and the home side began to panic. Roared on by the Scousers who had invaded every area of the ground, an equaliser seemed on the cards as Everton piled forward.

As the game entered its closing stages, the Blues won a corner, Arteta whipped it in and the immense Duncan Ferguson crashed a header past Mariano Barbosa. However, the Italian referee, Pierluigi Collina, blew his whistle and pointed not to the centre circle, but for a free kick to the home team. For what, it's never really been made clear. Then, in injury time, a deflated Everton conceded a breakaway goal that saw Villarreal triumph 4–2 on aggregate.

Collina's decision was baffling, and what makes it even worse is that by rights he should have hung up his whistle before he officiated this tie, but the Italian FA had raised the retirement age for referees by a year especially to accommodate him, such was his stature and reputation in Italy. Not on Merseyside, though.

— ONLY THE THIRD —

Ayegbeni Yakubu's hat-trick in the second leg of Everton's UEFA Cup tie with SK Brann in February 2008 was only the third scored in Europe by a Blues player. Alan Ball got the first, at home to IBK Keflavik in the European Cup in September 1970. There was then a 15-year wait until Andy Gray repeated the feat against the Dutch side Fortuna Sittard.

At this rate the next one is not due until around 2020.

— THE FOREIGN LEGION —

Players from beyond the British Isles to have played for Everton:

Australia	Jason Kearton, Tim Cahill
Brazil	Rodrigo, Anderson Silva de Franca
China	Li Tie, Li Wei Feng
Croatia	Slaven Bili
Denmark	Claus Thomsen, Thomas Gravesen, Peter Degn, Per Kroldrup
France	Mickael Madar, Olivier Dacourt, David Ginola
Ghana	Alex Nyarko
Israel	Idan Tal
Italy	Marco Materazzi, Alessandro Pistone, Matteo Ferrari
Ivory Coast	Ibrahima Bakayoko
Netherlands	Ray Atteveld, Andy van der Meyde, Sander Westerveld
Nigeria	Daniel Amokachi, Joseph Yobo, Victor Anichebe, Ayegbeni Yakubu
Norway	Thomas Myhre, Espen Baardsen, Bjarni Viðarsson
Poland	Robert Warzycha
Portugal	Abel Xavier, Nuno Valente, Manuel Fernandes
Russia	Andrei Kanchelskis
South Africa	David Murray, Steven Pienaar
Spain	Mikel Arteta
Sweden	Stefan Rehn, Anders Limpar, Niclas Alexandersson, Tobias Linderoth, Jesper Blomqvist
United States	Preki, Joe-Max Moore, Brian McBride, Tim Howard

— THE MARATHON MAN —

Ted Sagar was almost 42 years and 281 days old when he played his last top-flight game for Everton in November 1952. That made the Yorkshire-born goalkeeper the oldest man ever to represent the club and rounded off a career at Goodison that stretched back almost 23 years, another record.

His 463 league appearances stood as the club record until Neville Southall surpassed him, although it must be remembered that Sagar lost six years of his career thanks to the Second World War. During the hostilities he represented Northern Ireland in a wartime international. Given that he already had four England caps under his belt, he gained the rare distinction of turning out for two different international sides.

— HERE COME THE GIRLS —

Everton Ladies, formerly Leasowe Pacific, are one of the most successful teams in the women's game in England. They play their league matches at Marine FC's Rossett Park and feature a number of England internationals including Rachel Unitt, Fara Williams, Jill Scott, Emily Westwood and Rachel Brown. Their full honours list is as follows:

FA Women's Premier League National Division:
Winners: 1997/98
Runners-Up: 2005/06, 2006/07, 2007/08

FA Women's Cup:
Winners: 1988/89 (as Leasowe Pacific)
Runners-up: 1987/88 (as Leasowe Pacific), 2004/05

FA Women's Premier League Cup:
Winners: 2007/08
Runners-up: 1996/97, 1998/99

FA Women's Community Shield:
Runners-up: 2006/07

Liverpool County FA Cup:
Winners: 2008

— CELEBRITY BLUES —

Thankfully, professional Scousers such as Tarby and Cilla Black generally tend to latch onto the other lot. Still, there are some well known sorts who profess to be Blues, including:

Bill Dean	The actor, who appeared as one of the warders in *Scum* and for years as *Brookside*'s Harry Cross, was actually born Patrick Connolly but took his stage name in honour of his hero, Dixie.
Amanda Holden	Actress and ex-wife of Les Dennis. Incidentally, he came from a family of Blues but switched allegiance to Liverpool.
Leonard Rossiter	Comedy genius, star of *Rising Damp* and *The Fall and Rise of Reginald Perrin*. He never got where he was today by supporting anyone but the best.
Ed Stewart	Of *Crackerjack*.
Freddie Starr	Comedian, famous for a headline about him eating a hamster and turning up and acting the goat on chat shows in the 1980s.
Derek Hatton	Ex-Militant leader of Liverpool City Council now turned radio presenter.
James Barton	Founder of the Cream clubbing and music empire.
Gordon Honeycombe	The bald newsreader on breakfast television for years was also a playwright, responsible for penning *The Golden Vision*.
Ian Hart	Actor whose old-fashioned features have seen him turn up in lots of period films. Most recently appeared opposite Courteney Cox Arquette in the US TV series *Dirt*.

John Parrott	Gap-toothed snooker player and *Question of Sport* captain.
Simon O'Brien	Ex-*Brookside* actor and presenter of *Standing Room Only*.
Matt Dawson	England rugby union player and *Strictly Come Dancing* contestant.
Lee Mavers	Enigmatic frontman of the La's.
Elton Welsby	Sports presenter. Had the good fortune to be the anchor at Anfield when Arsenal clinched the league title with the last kick of the 1988/89 season.
Jennifer Ellison	Actress who appeared in *Brookside* before starring in the West End.
Gary Imlach	Sports presenter and writer. Son of ex-Blues coach Stewart Imlach, his book, *My Father and Other Working Class Heroes,* won the William Hill Sports Book of the Year in 2005.
Jimmy Mulville	Comedy actor, writer, producer and Everton shareholder. Also founder of Hat Trick Productions, the company that makes programmes like *Father Ted*, *Have I Got News for You* and *The Armstrong and Miller Show*.
Andy Burnham	Culture Minister in Gordon Brown's cabinet.

— TELEVISION DEBUT —

The opening match of the 1936/37 season saw Everton visit Arsenal on 29th August. This encounter has the distinction of being the first ever televised match in the country, and the small viewing public – there were fewer than 1,000 television sets in the country at this point – saw the Gunners triumph 3–2.

— EVERTON LEGENDS: DUNCAN FERGUSON —

Duncan Ferguson: sparked Fergiemania on Merseyside

Like Dave Hickson, another aggressive centre forward, Duncan Ferguson gave the crowd something to shout about when Everton were enduring one of the less celebrated periods of their history.

The Scottish striker often divided opinion amongst fans, as some think the fact that he achieved so little for someone with so many natural gifts was a criminal waste of talent. And in many ways they are probably right. Truly phenomenal in the air, hard as nails but blessed with excellent technique as well, Ferguson was unplayable when he was in the mood. Whether it was his attitude or the fact that he suffered with so many injuries though, those days when he was up for it could seem few and far between. However, his uncompromising nature, his contrariness – he refused to speak to the press – the way in which he attracted trouble on and off the pitch, and his knack of producing the goods on the big occasion, all lent him an aura that was irresistible to Evertonians. An Everton tattoo on his shoulder did him no harm either.

He initially arrived on loan from Glasgow Rangers in October 1994, along with Ian Durrant, and looked decent but not spectacular. That was the tail end of Mike Walker's disastrous time in charge and the arrival of the two Scots did nothing to save the hapless ex-Norwich manager. Joe Royle then took over and his first game was the Goodison derby. Stirred by the big occasion, Ferguson was immense, scoring the first goal and making a nuisance of himself in the build up to Paul Rideout's, the second in a 2–0 win that started the ball rolling for Royle and kept what looked like a relegation-bound club in the top flight. A legend was born, although perhaps a portent of things to come was his arrest for drink-driving hours after the match.

Undeterred, Royle made Ferguson's move permanent, in a £4.3 million deal, much to the delight of the supporters. In 1995 though they were horrified when he had to spend 44 days in Barlinnie Jail for a headbutt on Raith Rovers' John McStay – an incident that occurred when he was still at Rangers. To make matters worse, the Scottish FA declared that the 12-match ban they imposed on Ferguson would not start until he was released from jail. Eventually it was ruled that the ban could only be imposed in Scotland anyway, but by then Ferguson was so aggrieved that he retired from international football at the age of 24, with only seven caps to his name.

Controversially sold to Newcastle United in November 1998, Bill Kenwright brought the folk hero back to Goodison in August

2000 and Ferguson almost brought the house down with two goals against Charlton in his second 'debut'. Injuries plagued him again, as did disputes with David Moyes, but he seemed to mature at the very end of his career and was instrumental in helping the Blues qualify for the Champions League, especially when he scored the winner in a 1–0 win over Manchester United in April 2005.

He bowed out the following season with an equaliser in the final minutes of a home game against West Brom, stabbing home the rebound after almost spoiling the occasion by scuffing his penalty straight at the keeper. There was hardly a dry eye in the house as this famed hard man did his lap of honour, clearly emotional and giving his customary clenched fist salute for the last time.

Duncan Ferguson factfile
Born: Stirling, 27th December 1971
Appearances: 191 appearances (82 as substitute)
Goals: 72
Other clubs: Dundee United, Glasgow Rangers, Newcastle United
Full international appearances while at Everton: 3 for Scotland

— WHAT THEY SAID ABOUT DUNCAN FERGUSON —

"Put it this way, I'd rather be playing with him than against him."
Alan Shearer

"It might be interesting to note that since last March, when he recovered from that big operation on that nerve that was trapped in his buttock, I don't think he has missed a day's training apart from when he was quite ill and was a couple of weeks away. There was also that little problem with the manager when Duncan was away from the training ground a bit but otherwise he has been in training every day."
Everton physio, Mick Rathbone

"He has got a very sure touch for a big man and is unbelievably difficult to shake off the ball. He has got everything."
Gary McAllister

"We haven't really had a superstar here for a long time – someone who the fans can really look up to. But Duncan is the man for the job. He is a legend. It is Fergiemania!"
Dave Watson

"I hear big Fergie likes a few pints, loves to stay out late and chase the birds and gives a bit of lip in training. In my book he has all the ingredients of a good footballer."
Jim Baxter

— TEN DISTINCTIVE EVERTON HAIRSTYLES —

1. William Ralph Dean's tight curls that apparently earned him the somewhat politically incorrect nickname Dixie
2. Dave Hickson's quiff
3. Alan Biley's spiky Rod Stewart effort
4. Steve McMahon's wedge
5. Tiger McLaughlin's comb-over
6. Paul Bracewell's short back and sides
7. Peter Reid's 'Just for Men'
8. The indistinguishable baldies, Lee Carsley and Thomas Gravesen.
9. Alessandro Pistone's headband
10. Manuel Fernandes's cornrows

— YOUNG HOLT UNLIMITED —

In March 1890, tiny but tenacious centre half, Johnny Holt, became the first Everton player to represent England when he was called up to face Wales in Wrexham.

— EVERYBODY OUT! —

No one who was at Goodison on 9th November 1964 will forget it in a hurry. Don Revie's Leeds United, already with an uncompromising reputation further enhanced by the presence of ex-Blues star Bobby Collins in midfield, came to Everton expecting a battle. The atmosphere was hostile from the first whistle, with Jack Charlton commenting that the Everton crowd were "the worst before which I have ever played . . . there always seems to be a threatening attitude, a vicious undertone to their remarks."

Within the first four minutes, Everton full back Sandy Brown reacted to a tackle that left stud marks on his chest and threw a punch at Johnny Giles. He was predictably dismissed and that incident set the tone for the rest of a match that *The People* described as "spine-chilling".

Ten minutes before half-time, with Willie Bell and Derek Temple prostrate after an accidental clash and the pitch covered in missiles thrown by an incensed crowd, the referee Ken Stokes took the desperate step of ordering both sets of players from the field of play. He then lectured both sides in their changing rooms, threatening to abandon the match unless they calmed down.

Ultimately both teams returned to the field and the game was completed, with Leeds eventually winning 1–0.

— DEBUT SCORER —

Striker David Johnson is renowned for having two spells at Everton and also for enjoying a successful spell at Liverpool in between. The other thing he is remembered for was his propensity to score debut goals for the Blues. He managed to find the net in his first games in the FA Youth Cup, Central League, the Football League, the FA Cup, the League Cup and the European Cup. He also scored on his England debut in 1975, whilst an Ipswich player, and even managed to find the net in his first showing in the Merseyside derby too, the winner in fact at Goodison on 13th November 1971. However, he also scored for the Reds against Everton, making him the only player other than Peter Beardsley to have scored derby goals for both teams.

— FULL HOUSE —

Goodison attendances that broke the 70,000 mark:

Attendance	Opponents	Date	Competition
78,299	Liverpool	18th Sept 1948	First Division
77,920	Manchester United	14th Feb 1953	FA Cup 5th rd
76,839	Preston North End	28th Aug 1954	First Division
75,818	Blackburn Rovers	29th Jan 1958	FA Cup 4th rd
75,322	Wolves	27th Dec 1954	First Division
74,867	Burnley	27th Dec 1960	First Division
74,782	Charlton Athletic	28th Jan1959	FA Cup 4th rd
72,921	Tottenham	11th Feb 1950	FA Cup 5th rd
72,569	Wolves	31st Jan 1948	FA Cup 4th rd
72,488	Liverpool	22nd Sept1962	First Division
72,000	Liverpool	29th Jan 1955	FA Cup 4th rd
71,868	Manchester United	4th Sept 1957	First Division
71,587	Fulham	14th Feb 1948	FA Cup 5th rd
71,150	Liverpool	16th Sept 1950	First Division
71,088	Blackpool	7th April 1950	First Division
70,812	Liverpool	27th Aug 1949	First Division

— IT AIN'T HALF ALKMAAR —

Substitute James Vaughan's goal, clinching a 3–2 victory in the Blues' final group match in the 2007/08 UEFA Cup, also ended one of the longest running records in European football. The Dutch side AZ Alkmaar had not lost at home for 32 matches, going back over 30 years, despite hosting the likes of Sevilla, Werder Bremen, Villarreal and Liverpool in that time.

On the same night Jack Rodwell, at the age of 16 years and 248 days, become the youngest Everton player to feature in a European game.

— ANOTHER MOVE? —

While Goodison Park has served Everton Football Club as home for over a century and, in its time was widely regarded as one of the finest football stadia in the country, it has begun to show its age in recent years. The Park End was redeveloped in 1994, but even then many felt the club missed an opportunity by not making it two-tier and including more modern corporate boxes. The facilities for corporate entertainment are limited, with fewer than a dozen boxes across the front of the Main Stand, and a marquee in the car park behind the Park End currently being used to accommodate more diners – a situation that is far from ideal when compared to, say, the facilities just down the road at Old Trafford.

There are up to 4,000 seats with obstructed views at Goodison too, as the original designs incorporated a good many posts, as opposed to the more modern grounds where roofs are supported by way of a cantilever system instead. The catering and toilet facilities, particularly in the Bullens Road Stand, leave a great deal to be desired too.

Everyone seems to be agreed on those facts, but where there tends to be some difference in opinion is over how to find a solution. Redevelopment of Goodison would be the choice of almost all supporters, but the nature of the ground's landlocked locale, with houses on all but one side, means that has historically been difficult to achieve.

Movement to a new stadium seems to have been reluctantly accepted as the most realistic option then, but to where?

The 'Johnson Dome'

Back in 1997 chairman Peter Johnson conducted a ballot of the fans to see if they would be open to the idea of moving to a new arena – one that certainly looked impressive in the architect's drawings that were released to the public. The vote returned an overwhelming verdict in favour of a move, although questions were asked about the veracity of the poll because of doubts over how it was conducted. Nonetheless, Johnson had a mandate to relocate Everton, with Knowsley Golf Course, adjacent to the M57, widely believed to be his preferred destination. However, events overtook the move as Johnson left Everton under a cloud in November 1998.

The King's Dock

In 2000, Everton's new owners, led by Bill Kenwright, submitted proposals to build a 55,000-seater arena at the King's Dock, forming part of the city's regenerated waterfront and, crucially, making Everton's new home an integral feature of the world-famous Liverpool skyline. There was another vote, again resoundingly in favour, and this time there seemed less opposition to the plans as they really did seem to represent something iconic and bold for a club which, in recent times, has been accused of being far too conservative. In 2002, though, the whole project fell through as it became increasingly clear that Everton were not capable of raising the funds necessary to make the dream a reality.

Destination Kirkby

The latest plan for a new home for Everton involves a deal with retail giant Tesco, whose CEO Terry Leahy is an Evertonian, whereby the Blues' new stadium will form part of a large retail development on land adjacent to Kirkby town centre. Crucially, this would take Everton beyond the city boundaries, into neighbouring Knowsley, a fact that clearly had an influence on the result of yet another ballot – this time those in favour were only a small majority compared with the previous landslides. As of the summer of 2008, Everton and Tesco are trying to press ahead with the project although objections from neighbouring councils about the impact of the development have seen it called in by the government for a public enquiry.

An unthinkable option?

Inevitably, whenever the issue of a move is mentioned, the idea of sharing a new ground with close neighbours Liverpool always rears its head. For some, mainly neutrals, this is a no-brainer, and there are obvious powerful arguments against building two hugely expensive stadia in one city, one of which will be empty every other weekend. However, there seems to be little genuine appetite for this amongst fans of either team, regardless of how well things work for the big clubs in Munich or Milan.

— GREAT ESCAPES:
EVERTON 1 COVENTRY 1, 1998 —

After the dramatics of the last day of the 1993/94 campaign and the win against Wimbledon, many wondered whether Everton had the same stomach for a fight when they found themselves in similar circumstances four years later. Howard Kendall was back for his third spell at the club, but with limited funds – and some questions being asked about whether all his methods were still appropriate in an increasingly professional sport – the team struggled. Badly.

They were destroyed 4–0 by the newly crowned champions at Highbury on the penultimate weekend and so went into the final match, a home tie against Coventry City, in the relegation zone, one point behind Bolton Wanderers. The Trotters travelled to Stamford Bridge, to face a Chelsea team preoccupied with the upcoming Cup Winners' Cup Final, knowing that they only had to match Everton's result to stay up.

It looked desperate then, even worse than when they had faced Wimbledon, although instead of falling behind in the opening stages, this time it was Everton who struck early. On six minutes, Gareth Farrelly, a disappointing signing from Aston Villa, swung his right boot at Duncan Ferguson's knockdown and sent a blistering shot swerving high past Marcus Hedman and into the top corner of the Park End goal. Things got even better when news came through in the second half that Gianluca Vialli had put Chelsea ahead in London. Bolton would have to come from behind and win if Everton could retain their lead – one they had the chance to extend when Danny Cadamarteri was felled in the visitors' box with five minutes remaining.

Nick Barmby, under indescribable pressure, failed to emulate Graham Stuart, the hero of the Wimbledon game, and put his penalty too close to Hedman. Matters then got even worse when, with only two minutes remaining, Everton goalkeeper Thomas Myhre fumbled Dion Dublin's tame header into his net to level the scores. A last gasp equaliser for Bolton would send Everton down. Thankfully though, when news did come through of a goal at the Bridge it was a breakaway effort for Jody Morris, sealing the fate of the Trotters and of Everton.

After the match, as the emotionally drained fans cleared the pitch they had invaded amidst an almost apocalyptic thunderstorm, Kendall told the press that Everton would never again find themselves in this situation while he was in charge.

He left Everton for the final time that summer.

— MORE OF THE THINGS THEY SAID —

"He started crying but rather than saying 'Never mind' the fans just started shouting at him 'Stop crying, you soft get!'"
Dave Watson on Marco Materazzi's tears

"Everton Football Club breeds gentlemen."
Bob Latchford, following Brian Labone's death

"Once Everton has touched you nothing will be the same"
Alan Ball

"If Everton finish in a Champions League place, they'll play in the Champions League."
Mark Bright

"I have not been short of invitations to other clubs and have been received more warmly by Everton than I have by Liverpool."
Bill Shankly after his retirement

"That's a home win and an away draw inside four days. We've only got one more game in November, and if we win that I'm in grave danger of becoming Manager of the Month."
Mike Walker four days before being sacked

"We have signed Denmark's best player. Thomas Gravesen had some important offers from Italy and England but he only ever wanted to come to Real Madrid."
Real Madrid president **Florentino Pérez**

"I didn't have any offers at all except for the one from Madrid."
Thomas Gravesen

— RETURN THE BALL, PLEASE —

With the introduction of league football in 1888, Everton sought to become more organised as a football club, and one aspect of that was the issuing of a set of club by-laws. These included:

Every player, whether amateur or professional, shall appear in proper football costume both when practising and engaged in a match on behalf of the Club; and no member will be permitted to practise or play on the ground unless wearing the authorised football costume of the Club.

No practise, under any circumstances, will be permitted on days when matches are played, either before or after a match.

All reasonable commands of the Captain in the field must be promptly obeyed.

The Captain shall have the power to alter the position of the team, if during the progress of the match he thinks it advisable to do so.

The team shall be complete before leaving the dressing room and must come on the field in a body led by the Captain, at least five minutes before the advertised time of kick-off.

All articles for the use of the Members, provided by the Committee, are the property of the Club.

All boots, jerseys, football and pants shall be taken charge of by the storekeeper who shall be responsible for them and shall report to the Secretary every Monday as to their state and also to any loss or requirements.

The Captain shall return the ball to the storekeeper immediately on conclusion of the match.

— START AS YOU MEAN TO GO ON —

The first game that Everton played after changing their name from St Domingo FC was against a side called St Peters on 23rd December 1879. They won 6–0.

— FOG DAY AFTERNOON —

On 26th November 1904, Everton were leading away to Arsenal 3–1, thanks to two goals from Alex 'Sandy' Young and one from Harold Hardman. With only a quarter of an hour to go though, and the result seemingly in the bag, the referee abandoned the match due to thick fog, much to the understandable annoyance of the Everton players.

The match wasn't replayed until late April, the penultimate game of the season, and almost inevitably this time the result went the home side's way – a late Charlie Satterthwaite goal clinching a 2–1 result for the Londoners. The Blues won the final game of the season, at home to Nottingham Forest, but missed out on the title to Newcastle by a solitary point, which obviously underlined the significance of the lost result against the Gunners.

	P	W	D	L	F	A	GD	Pts
1 Newcastle	34	23	2	9	72	33	+39	48
2 Everton	34	21	5	8	63	36	+27	47

— TWO WINS, THREE TROPHIES —

Howard Kendall's Everton won the league twice in the mid-1980s but received three trophies. The triumph in 1984/85 saw them receive the rather modernist looking Canon League trophy, all shiny struts and golden ball. By the time they regained the title from Liverpool, two seasons later, the *Today* newspaper was the sponsor, but their trophy was a rather modest glass affair that had the look of a glorified paperweight about it. On the final day of that season then, an oddly fractious home game against Luton Town, Kevin Ratcliffe was presented with both the *Today* effort and the traditional league trophy too.

— FROM A LAND DOWN UNDER —

Thanks to his tenacity and his goalscoring record, Australian international midfielder Tim Cahill has proven to be one of the best buys made by Everton for years. He's no stranger to controversy though, with a couple of his goal celebrations in particular landing him in hot water. The first time came in September 2004, in only his second game for Everton following his transfer from Millwall. Having already been booked for a foul, Cahill scored what proved to be the winning goal at Manchester City and took his shirt off to celebrate. However, under the new rules introduced to curb overzealous celebrations, referee Steve Bennett brandished a second yellow card and sent Cahill off.

Even more of a storm was caused when Cahill scored in a 3–1 home win over Portsmouth on 2nd March 2008. He raced to the corner flag, crossing his wrists as if handcuffed, a gesture in support of his brother who had been jailed for assault. In the wake of the press furore that followed he had to issue an apology.

— A BOY NAMED SOO —

The Football League was suspended during the two World Wars and games were played on a regional basis. Guest players appeared for the often-depleted teams, and Everton were grateful to quite a few for turning out, including the likes of Johnny Carey, who would become the Blues' manager in the late 1950s, Aston Villa great Tom 'Pongo' Waring, and Frank Soo.

Soo, whose father was Chinese, was brought up in Liverpool although he made his name as a player with Stoke and Luton Town. He not only guested for Everton during the Second World War, he also played nine games for England, giving him the distinction of being the first ever non-white player to do so.

— SCANT CONSOLATION —

In the wake of the Heysel Stadium disaster and the subsequent banning of English clubs from Europe, the Screen Sports Super Cup was dreamt up in 1985 as a competition to be contested by the six clubs who initially missed out: Everton, Liverpool, Manchester United, Tottenham, Norwich City and Southampton.

The teams were split into two groups, with Everton, topping theirs ahead of Norwich and United, setting up a semi-final against Spurs. The fact that fewer than 18,000 fans turned up over the two legs gave an indication of the ill-conceived nature of the trophy – and any excitement that might have been generated by Everton's 3–1 triumph at Goodison, following a goalless game in London, was dampened by the fact that the final, against Liverpool, wasn't scheduled until the following season. That was another two-legged affair that the Reds won 7–2 on aggregate. Thankfully, the whole competition was then unceremoniously scrapped.

— TOTTENHAM 10 EVERTON 4 —

The most goals Everton have ever conceded in one match were the ten they shipped at White Hart Lane on 11th October 1958. Famously, Bill Nicholson was named as the new Tottenham manager shortly before the match and his new players certainly went about impressing the new boss in the right manner.

The Toffees were 6–1 down at half-time and although Jimmy Harris scored a hat-trick, Spurs were irresistible. Bobby Smith netted four times for the home side, Alf Stokes scored twice, while the rest were added by George Robb, Terry Medwin, Tony Harmer and John Ryden. A late Bobby Collins drive meant that the Blues put four past Tottenham keeper John Hollowbread – no mean feat away from home – but that was scant consolation for the barrage at the other end.

— THE ROAD TO ROTTERDAM —

Everton's complete record in the 1984/85 European Cup Winners'
Cup.

Round 1

19th Sept 1984	University College Dublin 0	Everton 0
2nd Oct 1984	Everton 1 (Sharp 11)	University College Dublin 0

Round 2

24th Oct 1984	Slovan Bratislava 0	Everton 1 (Bracewell 6)
7th Nov 1984	Everton 3 (Sharp 12, Sheedy 44 Heath 63)	Slovan Bratislava 0

Quarter-final

6th March 1985	Everton 3 (Gray 48, 74, 76)	Fortuna Sittard 0
20th March 1985	Fortuna Sittard 0	Everton 2 (Sharp 16, Reid 75)

Semi-final

10th April 1985	Bayern Munich 0	Everton 0
24th April 1985	Everton 3 (Sharp 48, Gray 73 Steven 86)	Bayern Munich 1 (Hoeness 38)

Final

15th May 1985	Everton 3 (Gray 57, Steven 72 Sheedy 85)	Rapid Vienna 1 (Krankl 83)

— NOTHING TO DO WITH DRUGS, HONEST —

It is something of a custom for Liverpool managers to make bizarre statements after derby matches, not least when the result has gone against them, but there have been fewer more embarrassing than Gerard Houllier's classic following the Reds' 3–2 victory at Anfield on 3rd April 1999. Unfounded rumours about Robbie Fowler's recreational habits had been doing the rounds of the city for some time and the Reds' striker had endured prolonged abuse from Everton fans as a result. So, when he scored a penalty in front of the Anfield Road end to cancel out Olivier Dacourt's opener, he decided to make fun of the Evertonians' jibes by getting down on his hands and knees and pretending to snort the white line that marked the edge of the box.

Not so, according to Monsieur Houllier though – he had a far more believable explanation. He said: "It was just a joke. The Metz players would get down behind each other and pretend to eat the grass. Rigobert [Song], who used to play for them, did it in training and we all had a laugh. Robbie did this in front of the Everton fans, but if the goal had been scored at the other end, he would have done it there.

"It was just a goal ceremony. It had nothing to do with drugs. At the moment, everything he does seems to be open to interpretation. When your heart is racing, maybe you don't think of the circumstances. We had a laugh about it in the dressing room. Robbie has been surprised by the reaction to this."

— ABANDONED—

The first ever abandoned league game that saw its result stand involved Everton. It occurred on 15th December 1888 at Stoke. With 15 minutes remaining, the referee abandoned the match due to impenetrable fog. As no goals had been scored it was ruled that the teams would take a point each.

— DUNCAN FERGUSON'S SENDINGS OFF —

Date	Result	Reason dismissed
14th Jan 1995	Arsenal 1 Everton 1	Pushed John Jensen to the ground
4th March 1995	Leicester 2 Everton 2	Allegedly elbowed Jimmy Willis
21st Sept 1996	Blackburn 1 Everton 1	Dissent: allegedly called ref David Elleray a "baldy bastard"
14th Feb 1998	Everton 1 Derby 2	Elbowed Paolo Wanchope
1st April 2002	Everton 3 Bolton 1	Punched Fredi Bobic
20th March 2004	Leicester 1 Everton 1	Two yellow cards for fouls on Steffen Freund
28th Dec 2004	Charlton 2 Everton 0	Elbowed Hermann Hreidarsson
31st Jan 2006	Wigan 1 Everton 1	Punched Paul Scharner in the stomach

The Scharner incident happened shortly after Ferguson had pushed Pascal Chimbonda in the face. According to Scharner: "Duncan Ferguson elbowed me in the neck three times and I was beginning to get a bit angry. I swore at him in Austrian and I know he couldn't possibly have understood it. Even so, he suddenly swung round and thumped me in the stomach. He got sent off, but I began to appreciate how he earned his reputation as a hard man. It was a nice punch, I have to say."

— THE PROFESSIONALS —

Paying players a wage was officially made legal in 1885, although clubs had surreptitiously offered financial inducements before that point. George Dobson was the first professional on the books at Everton, followed by George Farmer and the Scot, Alec Dick.

— CLASSIC MATCHES:
EVERTON 3 RAPID VIENNA 1, 1985 —

Finally, a European trophy. With their first league title in 15 years under their belts, Howard Kendall's emergent side travelled to the De Kuyp Stadium in Rotterdam on 15th May 1985, supremely confident of overturning the Austrian Cup winners, Rapid Vienna.

The Evertonians invaded Amsterdam and Rotterdam and the good-natured jaunt, with fans playing football with the Dutch police, is now legendary, especially given what happened at Heysel the following week.

The Blues dominated on the pitch although the game remained goalless at half-time. Just before the hour mark though, Graeme Sharp capitalised on a mistake at the back by Rapid and set up Andy Gray for the opener. Fifteen minutes later, Trevor Steven doubled the lead, finishing from close range following a Kevin Sheedy corner.

However, the Austrians looked like they might stage a comeback when their veteran star, Hans Krankl, pulled a goal back with an opportunist effort on 83 minutes. Before the travelling Blues had a chance to get nervous though, Sheedy went up the other end almost immediately and put the game beyond the Viennese once and for all.

"Everton were just too good for us. It's been a long time since we played anyone of their class. They are possibly the best side in the whole of Europe."
Hans Krankl

— THRASHING THE REDS —

Everton's biggest victory over Liverpool came way back on 9th April 1909, when they won 5–0 at Goodison Park. Bert Freeman scored twice while Tim Coleman, Joe Turner and Walter White added one apiece. Freeman, incidentally, was the first player to score over 30 league goals in one season for the Toffees.

— END OF THE ROAD —

Down the years Goodison Park has proven to be a tough place to come for teams defending impressive runs of form:

30th August 1969 – Leeds United

Don Revie's champions came to Everton for the seventh game of the 1969/70 season, on the back of a run of league games that had seen them unbeaten in 34 league matches. Not since October 1968 had the Yorkshiremen been turned over, and they looked to have extended that sequence when Billy Bremner and Allan Clarke cancelled out goals from Jimmy Husband and Joe Royle. However, Royle scored again to clinch a 3–2 win for the Blues who were on course to eventually bring the title back over the Pennines themselves.

20th March 1988 – Liverpool

Liverpool had matched Leeds United's record of going 29 games unbeaten from the start of the 1973/74 season when they came to Goodison, where they had already triumphed a month earlier in the FA Cup fifth round. A scrappy Wayne Clarke goal saw the Blues edge this one.

19th October 2003 – Arsenal

Arsène Wenger's top-of-the-table Gunners arrived in town looking to extend a record run of 30 matches unbeaten in the Premiership. All was going well for them when Freddie Ljungberg put them ahead, only for Tomasz Radzinski to equalise before half-time. The Canadian striker was then replaced by the 16-year-old Wayne Rooney with ten minutes of the game remaining. In the 90th minute he controlled a clearance in the Arsenal half, looked up and cracked in his first ever senior league goal, a stunning 30-yard effort that went in off the underside of David Seaman's crossbar.

— EVERTON LEGENDS: DAVE WATSON —

Dave Watson: rock solid

Dave Watson collected 12 England caps as well as a league championship and FA Cup winner's medal won with Everton, and a League Cup winner's medal acquired with Second Division Norwich City. His career is more glorious than most then, but still he is probably remembered with such great fondness by Evertonians more for the fact that he represented such solidity and determination on the field for the Blues during some of the club's very darkest days.

This old-fashioned defender started his career across the park at Anfield although he didn't make a first-team appearance before moving to Carrow Road in 1980, where he formed a formidable partnership with Steve Bruce. The Canaries were loath to lose him when he moved to Goodison for £900,000 in August 1986, although in truth the Everton fans struggled to see what all the fuss was about at first as Watson struggled for form. Replacing crowd favourite Derek Mountfield was always going to be tough too, but despite his early setbacks Watson persevered in trademark style until he and Kevin Ratcliffe began to operate as almost the textbook central defensive unit, the Englishman's strength and aerial power complementing the Welshman's electric pace. That partnership was key in bringing home the title for the second time in three years, but as that great side of the 1980s began to break up and the club slipped into decline, Watson found himself doing more work at the back than he perhaps expected when he first joined. He was the definition of the defensive rock, though, and it would be easy to imagine Everton slipping out of the top division if it had not been for the big Scouser's presence during the lowest periods of the mid-1990s, when the club twice came within a game of the drop.

Thankfully, it wasn't unremitting doom and gloom. Joe Royle's return to the club as manager saw a dramatic upturn in the Blues' form in 1994 and a bold push for the FA Cup the following year. Watson put in many skipper's performances along the way, not least in the quarter-final against a fancied Newcastle United when his header at the Gwladys Street proved the difference between the two sides. In the final, the way he marshalled the defence against Manchester United's second-half assault earned him the man-of-the-match award. To this date, he is still the last Everton captain to lift a major piece of silverware.

Such was the esteem in which he was held at the club, Watson was asked to take over the managerial reigns for the final seven games of the 1996/97 season following the resignation of Joe Royle. Three draws and one win during that stretch were enough to ensure that a weak Everton team again remained in the top flight.

Watson retired as a player in March 2001 to briefly manage Tranmere Rovers and is currently the youth team coach at Wigan Athletic.

Dave Watson factfile
Born: Liverpool, 20th November 1961
Appearances: 522 (6 as substitute),
Goals: 37
Other clubs: Liverpool, Norwich City
Full international appearances while at Everton: 6 for England

— AN IGNOMINIOUS START —

Everton have a proud tradition in the FA Cup, winning the competition outright on five occasions and finishing as runners-up on a further seven. However, their first foray, back in 1886, was less than glorious. They were drawn against Glasgow Rangers, on the one occasion that the Scots entered the English cup. Scotland had led the way in organised football in Britain and the Glasgow club were a formidable outfit. Indeed, they won 1–0 at Anfield, thanks to a goal from Charlie Heggie, but the result was rendered meaningless due to Everton's late realisation that they would be fielding ineligible players. Therefore the tie was forfeited and the match was played as a friendly.

If anything, the following season saw an even bigger debacle. Everton drew Bolton Wanderers and lost 1–0. However, an appeal saw the FA demand a replay as the Lancashire side were deemed to have fielded a player who registered too late to be eligible. The first replay at Anfield ended 2–2 and then another at Bolton was level again, this time 1–1. Eventually, Everton won through, 2–1, and went on to face Preston. However, in the meantime it was Bolton's turn to appeal and the FA ruled in their favour, agreeing that Everton had registered several of their professional players as amateurs. Therefore the tie was awarded to Bolton and the Preston result was scratched from the records. There were probably few complaints from Everton though, given that they had been battered 6–0.

— FULL MEMBERS —

You might have thought that the powers that be would have learned their lesson given the outright apathy that greeted the one and only season of the Screen Sports Super Cup. With no European football for English sides following the Heysel Stadium disaster, though, they were intent on filling the footballing calendar with games, and so was born the Full Members Cup, which later became known by the names of its sponsors, firstly Simod and then Zenith Data Systems.

Everton managed to do as well in these as they had in the Super Cup, getting to two finals, in 1989 and 1991. Even a day out at Wembley failed to excite the Evertonians though, and the take-up for tickets was unsurprisingly low. Those who chose not to bother were vindicated when the Blues lost 4–3 to Nottingham Forest after extra time in 1989. Even worse was the 4–1 bludgeoning they received at the hands of Crystal Palace in an ugly encounter in 1991.

— ALWAYS THERE —

When it comes to Everton records, two men, Dixie Dean and Neville Southall, tend to dominate. The Welshman especially when it comes to time spent out on the pitch representing the Blues, and so it comes as no surprise to see that he has had far more seasons as an ever present, playing every minute of every league match, than anyone else. Seven times he achieved that feat, in 1984/85, 1988/89, 1989/90, 1990/91, 1991/92, 1993/94 and 1995/96.

Another goalkeeper, Gordon West, had three ever-present seasons, as did Brian Labone, the record holder for an outfield player. He didn't miss a moment of the 1960/61, 1964/65 or 1968/69 campaigns

It's becoming an increasingly rare achievement, due to the demands of modern football and the greater willingness of managers to utilise their full squads, but still Everton's outstanding Nigerian international central defender, Joseph Yobo, was an ever present as recently as the 2006/07 season.

— CLASSIC MATCHES:
EVERTON 6 SUNDERLAND 4, 1935 —

Along with the 4–4 game against Liverpool in 1991, this fifth round encounter, played on 30th January 1935, is regarded as the most thrilling FA Cup tie ever played at Goodison.

There were worrying crushes inside and outside of the ground, but 60,000 fans managed to see Jackie Coulter put the Toffees 2–0 up within half an hour. Bert Davis pulled one back for the visitors, before Alex Stevenson looked to have put the Blues through to the next round when he made the score 3–1 with only 15 minutes left on the clock. Undeterred, the Black Cats fought on and got their reward when first Jimmy Connor beat Ted Sagar in the Everton goal and then Bobby Gurney forced extra time with an equaliser in the final seconds.

The drama was far from over, though. Coulter completed his hat-trick in the opening minutes of the first period of extra time, only for Connor to again peg Everton back. Albert Geldard, Everton's England winger, finally clinched the game though, scoring twice, to the delight of the enraptured home fans.

Ten goals in total then, and not one scored by the ubiquitous Dean for a change.

— TO VICTOR THE SPOILS —

Victor Anichebe's four goals in the 2007/08 UEFA Cup campaign elevated the Nigerian youngster to joint third in Everton's all-time European goalscoring chart. Fred Pickering is at the top, with six, followed by Andy Gray on five. Anichebe shares third with Graeme Sharp, Joe Royle, Alan Ball, Andy King, Andy Johnson and Mikel Arteta. What makes his achievement more notable though is that of the nine games he played in Europe, he started just the one, away at Alkmaar.

— ONE CLUB, ONE CITY, NO PLACE —

Everton weren't the only side to fall foul of the one-club-per-city rule in the Inter-Cities Fairs Cup, but still it comes as no surprise that they missed out before it was abandoned. The Blues finished fifth in 1967/68 but the ruling saw Liverpool, in third, entered into the competition as the city's sole representative. Newcastle, who finished as low as tenth in the league, also entered the cup and actually went on to win it.

— THE BEST EVER —

The champions of 1969/70 never went on to dominate the English game, but their legacy was that they set the bar extremely high for the following generations of Everton teams. Indeed, it wasn't until Howard Kendall put together his all-conquering side of the 1980s that anyone came close, and even then they didn't win as many games as Harry Catterick's second league title winners.

This was the team of Kendall, Harvey and Ball, the so-called Holy Trinity in midfield, but they were more than ably assisted by cracking players in their own right such as John Hurst, Jimmy Husband and Johnny Morrisey. The title came to Goodison in no small part thanks to the 23 goals of Joe Royle as well as Alan Whittle's 11, many of which came in crucial matches in the run-in.

Four straight wins at the start of the season, including Arsenal away and Manchester United both home and away got them off to a flier. Another eight straight victories in March and April, including a 2–0 victory at Anfield, then broke the hearts of the competition.

	P	W	D	L	F	A	Pts
Everton	42	29	8	5	72	34	66
Leeds United	42	21	15	6	84	49	57
Chelsea	42	21	13	8	70	40	55

— EVERY LITTLE HELPS —

Players who featured just once in the title-winning campaign of 1984/85:

Darren Oldroyd	Two minutes as a substitute at Nottingham Forest was the sum total of his Everton career. By the age of 21 he had slipped into non-league football with Southport.
Jason Danskin	Away to Luton on the final day was his only first team game for the Blues.
Derek Walsh	Walsh eventually carved a career out with Carlisle United and Hamilton Academical.
Neill Rimmer	He turned professional with Ipswich before playing almost 200 games for Wigan Athletic.
Johnny Morrisey Jr	The son of an Everton great, he went on to make a name for himself at Tranmere Rovers.

— NO PLACE LIKE HOME —

En route to their first FA Cup win at the end of the 1905/06 season, Everton were drawn at home in every round. First against West Brom, who were duly dispatched 3–1, and then Chesterfield, Bradford and Sheffield Wednesday who were overturned 4–3. The semi-final was the first time Everton had to travel in that season's competition, all the way down to Villa Park to face Liverpool of all teams. Walter Abbott and Harold Hardman's goals sealed victory and set up the final against Newcastle at Crystal Palace. Alex 'Sandy' Young scored the only goal there to finally win the cup after two previous disappointments at the final hurdle. They would return to the same venue the following season, hoping to hold on to the trophy, but Jack Sharp's goal wasn't enough to prevent them going 2–1 down to Sheffield Wednesday.

— AULD LANG SYNE —

Jack Taylor scored twice on New Year's Day 1897, giving Everton a 2–1 win at Sheffield United. Incredibly, it would take the best part of a century, until 1991, for the Toffees to win an away game on the first day of the year. Graeme Sharp's strike and an own goal from Jason Cundy brought the unwanted sequence to an end at Stamford Bridge. For good measure, the Blues won away on 1st January the following year as well, again 2–1, this time at the Dell.

— CLASSIC GOODISON PITCH-SIDE ADVERTISING HOARDINGS —

Higsons
Cutty Sark
Stilo Matchmakers
Plesseys
Eversell
Stanley Tools
Rizla
XL Crisps
John Wallwork
Merseyside County Council
Cream
Johnny Goggles

— THE FORGOTTEN SEMI-FINAL —

On 15th April 1989, Pat Nevin's goal in the FA Cup semi-final at Villa Park saw Everton triumph over Norwich City and booked the Blues' place at Wembley. However, what should have been a day for jubilation turned to horror when the events in the other semi-final at Hillsborough began to filter through. 96 Liverpool fans perished in the most horrific circumstances in Sheffield and a whole city went into mourning.

— TOP OF THE CHARTS, ONCE (POST-WAR) —

Players who have topped the Everton goalscoring charts just the once as of 2007/08:

Jim McIntosh, 1950/51 – 11 goals

A signing from Blackpool, McIntosh had seen much of his career blighted by the war and then was unlucky enough to miss the Seasiders' FA Cup Final against Manchester United because of an injury. He wasn't at Everton long, but he did make his mark with his goal haul in 1950/51.

Tony McNamara, 1956/57 – 10 goals

McNamara was one of the select band who have played for both the big clubs on Merseyside – he moved to Liverpool in 1957.

Eddie Thomas, 1957/58 – 15 goals

Thomas, who spent almost 11 years at Goodison, shared top spot in the scoring charts this season with Jimmy Harris.

Dave Hickson, 1958/59 – 22 goals

That's right, despite his heroics the Cannonball Kid was only ever top scorer on the one occasion.

Bobby Collins, 1959/60 – 14 goals

While diminutive in stature, the Pocket General was an immense influence on Celtic and Leeds United as well as Everton. Collins was quite simply one of the best and one of the most successful players of his generation.

David Johnson, 1971/72 – 11 goals

He of the many debut goals. Joe Royle's powers were on the wane and Bob Latchford was yet to arrive, so the top spot at Goodison was up for grabs in the early 1970s.

Joe Harper 1972/73 – 8 goals

The little Scot missed a penalty on his debut but still managed to hold off John Connolly and Joe Royle to finish in top spot.

Mick Lyons, 1973/74 – 9 goals

Mr Everton started his career as a centre forward before being converted into a defender. To this day, any Everton centre half who is pushed up in a desperate bid to snatch a goal is compared to Lyons.

Brian Kidd, 1979/80 – 17 goals
European Cup winner Kidd had an eventful season, finishing top scorer, netting the equaliser in the FA Cup semi-final against West Ham and then getting sent off in the same game.

Peter Eastoe, 1980/81 – 19 goals
Despite a decent goalscoring record, the well-travelled Eastoe was eventually swapped for the returning Andy King in July 1982.

Gary Lineker, 1986/86 – 40 goals
The Leicester goal-machine only spent one season at Goodison, but what a season it was. Evertonians will always wonder what might have been if he had stayed for longer.

Kevin Sheedy and Trevor Steven, 1986/87 – 16 goals
Adrian Heath scored 16 as well as the goals rained in and Everton swept to their last league title.

Peter Beardsley, 1991/92 – 20 goals
Often overlooked, the Geordie genius played in some awful Everton teams but he was always sublime. Both Liverpool and Everton were mad to let him go when they did.

Paul Rideout, 1994/95 – 14 goals
Something of an Indian summer for a player whose career seemed to have peaked as an England schoolboy. His winner against Manchester United in the FA Cup Final was clearly the pick of the bunch.

Andrei Kanchelskis, 1995/96 – 16 goals
The Ukrainian winger was like a force of nature when in full flow – truly breathtaking to behold. His two goals at Anfield will never be forgotten.

Gary Speed, 1996/97 – 10 goals
Joint top scorer with Duncan Ferguson, Speed's goals from midfield were crucial in keeping Everton from the drop.

Wayne Rooney, 2003/04 – 9 goals
In the youngster's last season before leaving for Manchester United he finished joint top scorer alongside his idol, Ferguson.

Tim Cahill, 2004/05 – 12 goals
An absolute steal from Millwall, there are few midfielders anywhere who can rival Cahill's ability to arrive late in the box and score crucial goals.

James Beattie, 2005/06 – 11 goals
The disappointing ex-Southampton striker enjoyed a purple patch between December and March but never looked totally convincing.

Andy Johnson, 2006/07 – 12 goals
The final goal in the 3–0 victory over Liverpool, when their Spanish goalkeeper fumbled Lee Carsley's shot on the line, allowing Johnson to score his second of the match, is possibly one of the funniest things ever seen at Goodison. "Reina drops keep falling on my head . . ."

Ayegbeni Yakubu 2007/08 – 21 goals
Awesome in his first season, the Nigerian looks destined to be the top scorer for as long as he remains an Everton player.

— DAYS OF YOUTH —

Everton have a reputation for developing young talent and that is reflected in their record in the FA Youth Cup. Manchester United and Arsenal have won the trophy more times than anyone else, but then Everton's three victories in the final puts them joint third alongside Liverpool, Ipswich, Aston Villa, West Ham and Tottenham.

FA Youth Cup winners
1965; 1984; 1998

Runners-up
1961; 1977; 1983; 2002

The win in 1984 completed a double, with the senior side winning the FA Cup proper. Arsenal in 1971, Coventry City in 1987 and Liverpool in 2006 are the only other clubs to have done the same.

— THE LAST FOR A WHILE —

Everton's most recent league title was secured when the Belgian-born Welshman, Pat Van Den Hauwe – the original 'Psycho' before Stuart Pearce ever earned the nickname – blasted home the only goal at Carrow Road on 4th May 1987. His wittily entitled Van Den Howitzer finally saw off the challenge of Liverpool, who for a long period had threatened to overtake the Blues for the second season in a row. With players like Neville Southall, Peter Reid, Kevin Sheedy, Graeme Sharp and Trevor Steven still in the side, bolstered by solid additions like Dave Watson, Paul Power and Wayne Clarke, experience and professionalism counted for a lot.

Howard Kendall's men often ground out wins and put together strings of victories that their opponents simply couldn't keep up with. Six straight wins over Christmas and New Year formed one such run, followed by another unbroken sequence of seven victories that started in March and included a famous goal from Clarke at Highbury. The younger brother of Leeds legend, Allan, controlled a miskicked clearance from John Lukic and lobbed the ball home from an outrageous distance to seal a 1–0 win against the Gunners.

	P	W	D	L	F	A	Pts
Everton	42	26	8	8	76	31	86
Liverpool	42	23	8	11	72	42	77

— A SCOUSE EVERTON XI —

Andy Rankin

Tommy Wright   Dave Watson   Brian Labone   Leighton Baines

Johnny Morrisey   Peter Reid   Colin Harvey   Ronnie Goodlass

Joe Royle   Wayne Rooney

— THE BACK PAGE OF THE ECHO —

Evertonians often talk about the good old days when the first you knew of the Toffees' link to a player was when he was pictured in the local paper holding up his new shirt or shaking hands with the manager. Unfortunately, though, there have been several cases where the Blues' pursuit of a transfer target has failed to run quite so smoothly:

Müller

Mike Walker was all but ready to announce the signature of the Brazilian World Cup-winning striker, only for negotiations to break down when his advisors realised that the figure being quoted for his salary was before deductions. Everton refused to pay his tax bill and so he got on a plane and went home.

Fabrizio Ravanelli

In July 1997, Everton agreed a fee with Middlesbrough for the silver-haired Italian striker. Television pictures showed him and a huge entourage of sharp-suited agents and accountants on Merseyside, but the Blues refused to budge on his astronomical wage demands and the deal eventually fell through.

Alan Shearer

This one didn't get as far as quibbling over personal demands as Everton rather peculiarly offered £12 million for the Blackburn striker *after* it was common knowledge that Newcastle United had already made a bid of £15 million.

Nigel Martyn

Everton had talks with the Crystal Palace keeper in July 1996 but failed to nail a deal down with him. The notorious story goes that they literally gave him directions to Elland Road instead. The Yorkshiremen signed him up and enjoyed the services of a magnificent player in the prime of his career. He did, however, eventually make it to Goodison in 2003 and, despite his advancing years, was still widely regarded as the best keeper seen at Everton since Neville Southall retired.

— MAD ABOUT THE ROY —

The standing joke about Roy Vernon was that his distinguished nose allowed him to smoke a cigarette in the shower without getting it wet. Despite the fact that he was fond of a smoke and never looked like the ideal of a top-class sportsman, the Welshman proved a shrewd acquisition when Everton landed him from Blackburn, in exchange for £27,000 and Eddie Thomas, in 1960. His powerful shooting and his pace made him the perfect foil for Alex Young. In fact, he consistently outscored the Golden Vision, topping the goalscoring charts at Goodison in his first four seasons and averaging pretty much a goal every other game before moving to Stoke in 1965.

His finest hour came in the final match of the 1962/63 season though, when Everton played host to Fulham. With the Blues unbeaten at home all season, Vernon scored a hat-trick in a 4–1 win that preserved that proud record but, more importantly, saw the title return to Goodison for the first time since the war.

"Taffy Vernon was about ten stone wet through. He looked about as athletic as Pinocchio."
Brian Labone

— POLL-AXED —

On 21st April 2000, Everton and Liverpool played out something of a scrappy and frantic game at Goodison that produced few chances at either end. In the dying seconds, Liverpool's goalkeeper, Sander Westerveld, took a quick free kick in the hope of launching one last attack. In his haste though, the Dutchman's punt struck the backside of the retreating Everton midfielder, Don Hutchison, and rebounded back into an empty net. As the majority of the 40,000 crowd went mad, though, referee Graham Poll blew his whistle, indicating an end to the match and, crucially, no goal.

The Everton players were incensed and their sense of injustice was only compounded when the Tring official's explanation, that he'd blown for full-time before the ball had crossed the line, was proved to be patently untrue.

"The referee took the easy way out."

Walter Smith

— EVERTON FANZINES —

When Skies Are Grey   Started in 1988, it's still going now and should be celebrating its 150th issue around Christmas 2008.

Blue Wail   Oddly enough the first issue came out on the very same day as WSAG #1, but it only lasted for a further two editions.

Speke From The Harbour   Originally founded by Irish Evertonians in 1989, Speke is still going strong under a local editor, Mark Staniford.

Gwladys Sings the Blues   On sale for a couple of seasons in the mid-1990s, its founder James Corbett went on to write an excellent history of the club, *Everton – The School of Science*, published in 2003.

Satis?   Another addition to the canon of fan-based writing that unfortunately only lasted for a couple seasons in the late 1990s.

Blueblood   George Orr's labour of love, which concentrates on Everton history and is never anything but fascinating, is on sale from outside the Winslow pub on matchdays. George has also written three excellent books, *Everton in the Sixties*, *Everton in the Seventies* and *Everton in the Eighties*.

— EVERTON LEGENDS: JOE ROYLE —

Joe Royle: loyal servant to the cause

A Scouser through and through, big Joe Royle joined the Blues as an apprentice in July 1964. Even in his wildest dreams, though, he would not have been able to imagine the impact he would make at the club or how quickly he would be making it. Aged 16 years and 282 days, he became the first ever 16-year-old to play in the league for Everton when started ahead of the axed Alex Young at Blackpool in January 1966.

Royle returned to the reserves for a spell after that, but his exceptional aerial ability and eye for goal meant that it wasn't too long before he made the number 9 shirt his own. He scored his first two senior goals at home to Chelsea at the tail end of the 1966/67 season but it was the second half of the following campaign where he came into his own. Indeed, he would be the club's highest goalscorer on five occasions as he notched up 119 goals, the fifth highest total ever. That tally would undoubtedly have been much higher too had it not been for the serious back injuries he suffered and the ensuing operations. They hampered his career and as a result Everton let him go to Manchester City in December 1974 for £200,000.

Perhaps fittingly, he scored his last ever league goal at Goodison, when he returned with Norwich City in the early 1980s, but his association with his hometown club was far from over.

Royle moved into management with Oldham Athletic in 1982 and enjoyed remarkable success with the Lancashire club. On miniscule budgets he took them to the top division in 1991, where they stayed for three seasons, and also led them to a League Cup Final and the verge of the FA Cup Final as well, only to be denied by a famous Mark Hughes goal for Manchester United.

He was lured back to Everton as manager in November 1994, and not a minute too soon. Everton were doomed under the hopelessly out of his depth Mike Walker, but Royle instantly instilled confidence and a certain belligerence into the club. Ever the realist, he understood that survival was more important than the club's School of Science heritage and the direct, in-your-face style, built around men like Duncan Ferguson, Barry Horne and Joe Parkinson earned his team the nickname the Dogs of War.

Along with Premier League survival came success in the FA Cup in 1995, at the end of Royle's first season. Probably the most enduring image of the final is the one of Royle on the touchline, turning to Alex Ferguson and winking when Paul Rideout scored the game's only goal.

The following season, with new club-record signing Andrei Kanchelskis utterly unstoppable, Everton finished sixth in the league and the future looked rosy. However, a spate of injuries decimated the team over Christmas 1996 and a run of six straight league defeats piled the pressure on Royle who was also embroiled in a bitter and distracting row with sections of the local press. A horrible home defeat by Bradford in the FA Cup only exacerbated matters and then, in March 1997, after a dispute with the chairman Peter Johnson over transfer targets, Royle left the club 'by mutual consent'.

It was a disappointing way for such a good manager to depart, and for years fans have wondered, in the light of how his successors fared until the arrival of David Moyes, whether things might have turned out better if he had been given more time to turn things around.

An immensely likeable man, Royle has done reasonably well in charge of Manchester City and Ipswich Town since then and is always warmly welcomed whenever he returns home to Goodison Park.

Joe Royle factfile
Born: Liverpool, 8th April 1948
Appearances: 273 (3 as substitute)
Goals: 119
Other clubs: Manchester City, Bristol City, Norwich City
Full international appearances while at Everton: 2 for England

— YOU'VE GOT TO FANCY EVERTON —

Some classic John Motson commentary from Everton matches:

"Its Arsenal 0 Everton 1, and the longer it stays like that the more you've got to fancy Everton"

"He got behind Lawrenson there, did Sharp."

"It's going to fall for Andy King!"

"Reid's cross, Gray!"

— NORTH OF THE BORDER —

Everton have played in some quite obscure competitions against Scottish teams down the years, including:

The British League Cup
Organised as a fundraiser in aid of the Ibrox Disaster Fund, this mini-tournament in 1902 featured teams from England and Scotland. After a goalless draw at Goodison, Glasgow Rangers beat Everton 2–1 in a replay at Celtic Park.

The Empire Exhibition Trophy
A solid silver replica of the Tait Tower, the centrepiece of the 1938 British Empire Exhibition in Glasgow, was the prize in this tournament featuring four teams from England and four from Scotland. The Toffees beat Rangers and Aberdeen to get to the final where they were defeated 1–0 by Celtic in front of 82,000 fans at Ibrox Park.

The British Championship
The champions of England, Everton, faced the champions of Scotland, Glasgow Rangers, in a two-legged affair at the tail end of 1963. Ironically it was two of Everton's Scots who were key in earning victory for the English club though – Alex Scott and Alex Young both scored in a 3–1 triumph at Ibrox and Young netted again, this time in a 1–1 draw, when the sides faced each other at Goodison.

The Dubai Championship Cup
Played in Dubai in December 1987, this was more or less a replay of the British Championship. Everton led thanks to Kevin Sheedy and Dave Watson before a late comeback from Rangers took the match to penalties. Fifteen were slotted successfully before Chris Woods saved Ian Snodin's and won the trophy for the Scots.

— DIXIE'S 60 —

A change in the offside law in 1925, requiring only two players between the attacker and the goal instead of three, instantly caused the number of league goals scored to increase dramatically. Initially Second Division Middlesbrough's George Camsell was the biggest beneficiary, bagging a massive 59 goals in the 1926/27 season. However, Everton's Dixie Dean set about besting that record the very next season, and in the top division too, as he was apparently fond of reminding people.

Dean scored in the opener against Sheffield Wednesday and then in each of the next eight matches, with doubles against Birmingham, Newcastle, Huddersfield and Tottenham, and an incredible five-goal haul at home to Manchester United. His hot streak was halted briefly by Liverpool at Goodison – typical – but then Dean had his revenge when he scored a hat-trick at Anfield on 25th February 1928.

With two games remaining in the season his tally stood at 53 goals – seven short of beating Camsell's record. Four goals at Turf Moor against Burnley on the penultimate weekend of the season then left him needing a hat-trick against Arsenal, on 5th May 1928, to write his name in the history books.

Everton were already champions and the league trophy was to be presented at the end of the match, incidentally Charlie Buchan's last ever appearance for the Gunners. However, the crowd of 48,000 – although reports suggest that many more than the official figure were crammed in – were only there to see if Dixie could break the record. The game started more dramatically than any of them could have imagined though, as Arsenal took the lead and then Dean replied twice, once from the penalty spot, and all within the first three minutes.

Camsell's record was equalled then, with almost the entire match left to play. However, anxiety on Everton's part, and resolute defending by the visitors, meant that chances started becoming scarce for Dean. With just under ten minutes remaining, Alec Troup sent over a corner and the Everton centre forward rose in his customary fashion, bulleting a header past the Arsenal goalkeeper, Dr Jimmy Paterson.

Even a late equaliser for the visitors couldn't dampen the spirits of the Evertonians who cheered until the final whistle. They knew they had seen history being made.

The full rundown of how he did it:

Date	Opponents	Score	Goals (tally)
27th Aug 1927	Sheffield Wednesday (a)	4–0	1 (1)
3rd Sept 1927	Middlesbrough (a)	2–4	1 (2)
5th Sept 1927	Bolton Wanderers (a)	1–1	1 (3)
10th Sept 1927	Birmingham City (h)	5–2	2 (5)
14th Sept 1927	Bolton Wanderers (h)	2–2	1 (6)
19th Sept 1927	Newcastle United (a)	2–2	2 (8)
24th Sept 1927	Huddersfield Town (h)	2–2	2 (10)
1st Oct 1927	Tottenham Hotspur (a)	3–1	2 (12)
8th Oct 1927	Manchester United (h)	5–2	5 (17)
29th Oct 1927	Portsmouth (a)	3–1	3 (20)
5th Nov 1927	Leicester City (h)	7–1	3 (23)
12th Nov 1927	Derby County (a)	3–0	2 (25)
26th Nov 1927	Bury (a)	3–2	2 (27)
10th Dec 1927	Aston Villa (a)	3–2	3 (30)
24th Dec 1927	Arsenal (a)	2–3	1 (31)
26th Dec 1927	Cardiff (h)	2–1	2 (33)
31st Dec 1927	Sheffield Wednesday (a)	2–1	2 (35)
2nd Jan 1928	Blackburn Rovers (a)	2–4	2 (37)
7th Jan 1928	Middlesbrough (h)	3–1	2 (39)
4th Feb 1928	Huddersfield Town (a)	1–4	1 (40)
25th Feb 1928	Liverpool (a)	3–0	3 (43)
24th March 1928	Derby County (h)	2–2	2 (45)
6th April 1928	Blackburn Rovers (h)	4–1	2 (47)
7th April 1928	Bury (h)	1–1	1 (48)
14th April 1928	Sheffield United	3–1	2 (50)
18th April 1928	Newcastle United (h)	3–0	1 (51)
21st April 1928	Aston Villa (h)	3–2	2 (53)
28th April 1928	Burnley (a)	5–3	4 (57)
5th May 1928	Arsenal (h)	3–3	3 (60)

— HANDBALL HANSEN —

Rather peculiarly, given the rich cup tradition of both Merseyside clubs, Everton and Liverpool had never faced each other at Wembley until the League Cup Final of 1984. Needless to say, if there was going to be a ropy decision in such an encounter then it wouldn't be in Everton's favour.

In the early stages of the match, Bruce Grobbelaar, who would have many of his wildest moments in derby games, gifted the ball to the alert Adrian Heath who lofted a shot towards the gaping goal. However, Alan Hansen got back and juggled the ball off the line like Meadowlark Lemon, only for referee Alan Robinson to inexplicably wave play on.

The match eventually finished goalless and a great strike from Graeme Souness – with his foot – saw the Reds win the replay 1–0 at Maine Road.

— WHEN SKIES ARE GRAY —

Everton never lost a match in which Scottish striker Andy Gray scored. Now, he may have only scored 22 goals, but they were often crucial and many see his arrival at Goodison in November 1983 as the catalyst for all that was achieved by Everton's most successful side ever.

Previously the subject of the most expensive British transfer when he moved from Aston Villa to Wolves in 1979, Gray was seen as well past his best, due to a number of serious injuries, when Howard Kendall shelled out £250,000 for him.

He scored the Blues' second goal in a 2–1 win at Notts County in the FA Cup quarter-final in his first season before netting the second at Wembley in the 1984 final. Gray was always a feisty, controversial figure and that goal against Watford, to seal a 2–0 win and make Elton John cry, raised some eyebrows as his challenge on the keeper, Steve Sherwood, was a bit of a throwback to Dixie Dean's era.

The following season, as the Toffees took their first title since 1969/70, he scored important goals in the league but it was the five he bagged in the Cup Winners' Cup, including strikes in both the semi-final and final, that were pivotal in securing the club's only European honour.

It was no wonder then that Kendall's decision to let him go that summer and replace him with Gary Lineker was seen as a controversial one at the time.

— THE FINAL WORD —

"Remember lads, one Blue is worth twenty Reds"
Brian Labone

BIBLIOGRAPHY

The Blue Correspondence: Everton Season 1888–89 – Billy Smith

Colin Harvey's Everton Secrets – Colin Harvey and John Keith

Everton Player by Player – Ivan Ponting

Everton: The Official Guide 2008 – Gavin Buckland

Everton: School of Science – James Corbett

Everton: The Ultimate Book of Stats and Facts – Dave Ball and Gavin Buckland

Everton: Strange But Blue – Gavin Buckland

Goodison Glory: The Official History – Ken Rogers

The Road to Rotterdam – Mark O'Brien

The Toffees: Day-to-Day Life at Goodison Park – Graham Betts

Virgin Blues: Everton – 100 Seasons at the Top – David H France and David Prentice

Who's Who of Everton – Tony Matthews

The Evertonian

The official matchday programme

Daily Post

Liverpool Echo

www.bluekipper.com

www.evertonfc.com

www.evertonresults.com

www.toffeeweb.com

— EVERTON'S LEAGUE RECORD 1888–2008 —

Season	P	W	D	L	GF	GA	W	D	L	GF	GA	Pts	Pos
Football League													
1888/89	22	8	0	3	23	14	1	2	8	12	32	20	8th
1889/90	22	8	2	1	40	15	6	1	4	25	25	31	2nd
1890/91	22	9	0	2	39	12	5	1	5	24	17	29	1st
1891/92	26	8	2	3	32	22	4	2	7	17	27	28	5th
First Division													
1892/93	30	9	3	3	44	17	7	1	7	30	34	36	3rd
1893/94	30	11	1	3	63	23	4	2	9	27	34	33	6th
1894/95	30	12	2	1	47	18	6	4	5	35	32	42	2nd
1895/96	30	10	4	1	40	17	6	3	6	26	26	39	3rd
1896/97	30	8	1	6	42	29	6	2	7	20	28	31	7th
1897/98	30	11	3	1	33	12	2	6	7	15	27	35	4th
1898/99	34	10	2	5	25	13	5	6	6	23	28	38	4th
1899/00	34	11	1	5	30	15	2	6	9	17	34	33	11th
1900/01	34	10	4	3	37	17	6	1	10	18	25	37	7th
1901/02	34	11	2	4	31	11	6	5	6	22	24	41	2nd
1902/03	34	10	2	5	28	18	3	4	10	17	29	32	12th
1903/04	34	13	0	4	36	12	6	5	6	23	20	43	3rd
1904/05	34	14	2	1	36	11	7	3	7	27	25	47	2nd
1905/06	38	12	1	6	44	30	3	6	10	26	36	37	11th
1906/07	38	16	2	1	50	10	4	3	12	20	36	45	3rd
1907/08	38	11	4	4	34	24	4	2	13	24	40	36	11th
1908/09	38	11	3	5	51	28	7	7	5	31	29	46	2nd
1909/10	38	8	6	5	30	28	8	2	9	21	28	40	10th
1910/11	38	12	3	4	34	17	7	4	8	16	19	45	4th
1911/12	38	13	5	1	29	12	7	1	11	17	30	46	2nd
1912/13	38	8	2	9	28	31	7	5	7	20	23	37	11th
1913/14	38	8	7	4	32	18	4	4	11	14	37	35	15th
1914/15	38	8	5	6	44	29	11	3	5	32	18	46	1st
1915–19	League football suspended due to the First World War												
1919/20	42	8	6	7	42	29	4	8	9	27	39	38	16th
1920/21	42	9	8	4	40	26	8	5	8	26	29	47	7th
1921/22	42	10	7	4	42	22	2	5	14	15	33	36	20th
1922/23	42	14	4	3	41	20	6	3	12	22	39	47	5th
1923/24	42	13	7	1	43	18	5	6	10	19	35	49	7th

1924/25	42	11	4	6	25	20	1	7	13	15	40	35	17th
1925/26	42	9	9	3	42	26	3	9	9	30	44	42	11th
1926/27	42	10	6	5	35	30	2	4	15	29	60	34	20th
1927/28	42	11	8	2	60	28	9	5	7	42	38	53	1st
1928/29	42	11	2	8	38	31	6	2	13	25	44	38	18th
1929/30	42	6	7	8	48	46	6	4	11	32	46	35	22nd

Second Division

| 1930/31 | 42 | 18 | 1 | 2 | 76 | 31 | 10 | 4 | 7 | 45 | 35 | 61 | 1st |

First Division

1931/32	42	18	0	3	84	30	8	4	9	32	34	56	1st
													(Champions)
1932/33	42	13	6	2	54	24	3	3	15	27	50	41	11th
1933/34	42	9	7	5	38	27	3	9	9	24	36	40	14th
1934/35	42	14	5	2	64	32	2	7	12	25	56	44	8th
1935/36	42	12	5	4	61	31	1	8	12	28	58	39	16th
1936/37	42	12	7	2	56	23	2	2	17	25	55	37	17th
1937/38	42	11	5	5	54	34	5	2	14	25	41	39	14th
1938/39	42	17	3	1	60	18	10	2	9	28	34	59	1st
1939–46	League football suspended due to the Second World War												
1946/47	42	13	5	3	40	24	4	4	13	22	43	43	10th
1947/48	42	10	2	9	30	26	7	4	10	22	40	40	14th
1948/49	42	12	5	4	33	25	1	6	14	8	38	37	18th
1949/50	42	6	8	7	24	20	4	6	11	18	46	34	18th
1950/51	42	7	5	9	26	35	5	3	13	22	51	32	22nd

Second Division

1951/52	42	12	5	4	42	25	5	5	11	22	33	44	7th
1952/53	42	9	8	4	38	23	3	6	12	33	52	38	16th
1953/54	42	13	6	2	55	27	7	10	4	37	31	56	2nd

First Division

1954/55	42	9	6	6	32	24	7	4	10	30	44	42	11th
1955/56	42	11	5	5	37	29	4	5	12	18	40	40	15th
1956/57	42	10	5	6	34	28	4	5	12	27	51	38	15th
1957/58	42	5	9	7	34	35	8	2	11	31	40	37	16th
1958/59	42	11	3	7	39	38	6	1	14	32	49	38	16th
1959/60	42	13	3	5	50	20	0	8	13	23	58	37	16th
1960/61	42	13	4	4	47	23	9	2	10	40	46	50	5th
1961/62	42	17	2	2	64	21	3	9	9	24	33	51	4th
1962/63	42	14	7	0	48	17	11	4	6	36	25	61	1st

1963/64	42	14	4	3	53	26	7	6	8	31	38	52	3rd
1964/65	42	9	10	2	37	22	8	5	8	32	38	49	4th
1965/66	42	12	6	3	39	19	3	5	13	17	43	41	11th
1966/67	42	11	4	6	39	22	8	6	7	26	24	48	6th
1967/68	42	18	1	2	43	13	5	5	11	24	27	52	5th
1968/69	42	14	5	2	43	10	7	10	4	34	26	57	3rd
1969/70	42	17	3	1	46	19	12	5	4	26	16	66	1st
1970/71	42	10	7	4	32	16	2	6	13	22	44	37	14th
1971/72	42	8	9	4	28	17	1	9	11	9	31	36	15th
1972/73	42	9	5	7	27	21	4	6	11	14	28	37	17th
1973/74	42	12	7	2	29	14	4	5	12	21	34	44	7th
1974/75	42	10	9	2	33	19	6	9	6	23	23	50	4th
1975/76	42	10	7	4	37	24	5	5	11	23	42	42	11th
1976/77	42	9	7	5	35	24	5	7	9	27	40	42	9th
1977/78	42	14	4	3	47	22	8	7	6	29	23	55	3rd
1978/79	42	12	7	2	32	17	5	10	6	20	23	51	4th
1979/80	42	7	7	7	28	25	2	1	9	15	26	35	19th
1980/81	42	8	6	7	32	25	5	4	12	23	33	36	15th
1981/82	42	11	7	3	33	21	6	6	9	23	29	64	8th
1982/83	42	13	6	2	43	19	5	4	12	23	29	64	7th
1983/84	42	9	9	3	21	12	7	5	9	23	30	62	7th
1984/85	42	16	3	2	58	17	12	3	6	30	26	90	1st
1985/86	42	16	3	2	54	18	10	5	6	33	23	86	2nd
1986/87	42	16	4	1	49	11	10	4	7	27	20	86	1st
1987/88	40	14	4	2	34	11	5	9	6	19	16	70	4th
1988/89	38	10	7	2	33	18	4	5	10	17	27	54	8th
1989/90	38	14	3	2	40	16	3	5	11	17	30	59	6th
1990/91	38	9	5	5	26	15	4	7	8	24	31	51	9th
1991/92	42	8	8	5	28	19	5	6	10	24	32	53	12th

Premier League

1992/93	42	7	6	8	26	27	8	2	11	27	28	53	13th
1993/94	42	8	4	9	26	30	4	4	13	16	33	44	17th
1994/95	42	8	9	4	31	23	3	8	10	13	28	50	15th
1995/96	38	10	5	4	35	19	7	5	7	29	25	61	6th
1996/97	38	7	4	8	24	22	3	8	8	20	35	42	15th
1997/98	38	7	5	7	25	27	2	8	9	16	29	40	17th
1998/99	38	6	8	5	22	12	5	2	12	20	35	43	14th
1999/00	38	7	9	3	36	19	5	5	9	23	28	50	13th

2000/01	38	6	8	5	29	27	5	1	13	16	32	42	16th
2001/02	38	8	4	7	26	23	3	6	10	19	34	43	15th
2002/03	38	11	5	3	28	19	6	3	10	20	30	59	7th
2003/04	38	8	5	6	27	20	1	7	11	18	37	39	17th
2004/05	38	12	2	5	24	15	6	5	8	21	31	61	4th
2005/06	38	8	4	7	22	22	6	4	9	12	27	50	11th
2006/07	38	11	4	4	33	17	4	9	6	19	19	58	6th
2007/08	38	11	4	4	34	17	8	4	7	21	16	65	5th

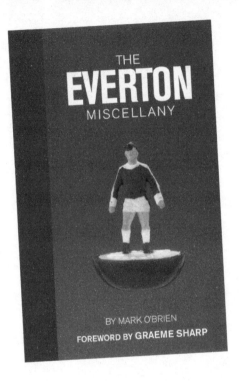